# HTML & CSS

## *Learn the Fundamentals in 7 Days*

MICHEAL KNAPP

58950767

# TABLE OF CONTENTS

# INTRODUCTION

I want to thank you and congratulate you for downloading the book, *"HTML and CSS for Beginners"*.

This book contains detailed information on what HTML and CSS are. It clearly explains what these two languages are all about, how they started, when they were developed, and what their purposes are. More importantly, it discusses the elements involved in both languages.

If you are new to programming, you will have no problem reading and grasping what is written in this book. The terms used are easily comprehendible even by people who are not used to using computer programming-related jargon. Even if it is your first time to create a website, you will also not be confused because the fundamentals are well covered and the steps you need to do are thoroughly discussed.

This book is also pretty short to be read in one sitting, but long enough to have every vital topic covered. Since you are a beginner, the examples included in this book are simple and basic. It covers just the topics you need to get started with programming and creating websites. There is no need for you to try writing codes that are complex. You can get to that once you are familiar with the fundamentals and already have an excellent grasp of HTML and CSS.

The elements of the two languages are discussed, starting from the fundamentals to the advanced. The most practical topics are covered to help you start coding right away. In fact, you can practice coding as you read the book.

There are basic sample programs that you can try on your computer. Type the codes and see how they run. You can also modify the codes to see their effects on the output. Feel free to tweak the codes to achieve your desired outputs as well as to get used to using the right codes.

There are also frequently asked questions (FAQ) that give you more insight on HTML and CSS. So, if you are curious about something but you do not have anyone to ask, you may see the answer in this book. The questions commonly asked by beginners are answered here.

This book also contains longer sample programs to help you understand HTML and CSS better. If you think that you can handle running longer programs, you can practice with the examples. They are not too long, but they are long enough to show you the differences that each block of code makes. This book also gives you tips with regard to what you should use and what you should not use when you write your codes.

The purpose of this book is to help you understand and know more about Web design and development using HTML and CSS. It is especially designed with a beginner like you in mind. In general, there are two types of people who would read this book: those who wish to learn how they can design and create a website from scratch and those who already has a website and wish to have more control over its pages.

In this day and age, everything is easily accessible. Thanks to the Internet, you can even create a website using the tools available online. There are free and paid versions, so you can make the most of your available options. You can create a website using an e-commerce platform, a content management system, or a blogging software. Nevertheless, you cannot have full control over it unless you make use of CSS and the elements discussed in this book.

That is the beauty of creating your own program. You get to decide every aspect of it. You get to have control of everything, from the start to the finish. You are the author of the program, so you have the power to tweak it according to your liking. You do not have to conform to someone else's rules because you can create your own. Whatever your imagination creates, you can turn it into reality.

It may seem daunting to create a website at first. This is especially true if you are not tech savvy or you do not possess much technical knowledge. All those lines of codes can make you dizzy and confused. You may even become fearful of crashing your own system if you make a mistake in your program.

Then again, the good thing about using HTML and CSS is that you can easily learn the languages even if you are a beginner and have no previous knowledge of programming. You can also test small batches of codes to see how they work. There are websites that allow you to test codes in different languages, making programming much easier for you.

HTML and CSS are not as complicated as other computer languages. They are perfect for anyone who has a basic understanding of how computers and the Internet work. HTML and CSS are actually great for young students who are just starting to write programs.

What's more, you do not need any fancy or expensive equipment. You can create a nice website using a text editor and a Web browser – both of which are already installed in your computer. If you want to find another text editor or browser, however, you can download one from the Internet. You have a lot of choices to choose from.

Understanding both HTML and CSS can help anybody who works with the Internet. Web designers can produce more usable and attractive websites while Web editors can produce better content. Likewise, Internet marketers can reach out to their target audience more efficiently while managers can commission much better websites and gain better results from their teams.

There is truly something for everybody with HTML and CSS. Also, if you are looking forward to a career in information technology, learning these languages would put you in a great advantage. Once you become adept at HTML and CSS, learning other programming languages would be a piece of cake.

Thanks again for downloading this book, I hope you enjoy it!

# CHAPTER 1:
# INTRODUCTION TO HTML AND CSS

## Fundamentals

### *Introduction to HTML*

HTML is a computer language specifically designed for creating websites. Such websites can be visited by anyone regardless of their location or time zone. As long as you have an Internet connection, you can visit websites.

The computer language is easy to learn. Its fundamentals can actually be grasped in just one sitting. Even though it is simple, it is effective and powerful. It is also continuously going through revisions in order to meet the requirements and demands of users.

HTML stands for Hyper Text Markup Language. Hyper Text is a method used to move across the Internet. You can click on hyperlinks, which are special texts that move you towards the next page. It is called hyper because it is not linear. In other words, you can move towards any location on the Internet at any time you desire simply by clicking on links.

It is a standard markup language for making Web pages. It describes Web page structure using markup. The HTML tags does markup to the texts inside them. Simply put, they mark it as a specific type of texts, such as italicized or bold. The elements of HTML are basically the building blocks of HTML pages. Its elements are represented by tags and its tags label content with heading, table, and paragraph among other.

Even though browsers do not generally display HTML tags, they use these tags to render the contents of pages.

*Frequently Asked Questions (FAQ)*

**How does HTML work?**
The computer language has a series of short codes that are typed into a text file. These become the tags of the HTML. The text is saved as an HTML file and is viewed using a browser such as Internet Explorer. The browser reads the file and then translates the text to a visible form that renders the page as the programmer intended.

When you write HTML codes, you have to use tags correctly. You can use a powerful graphical editor or a rudimentary text editor to create your pages.

**What do HTML tags do?**
Tags separate normal texts from codes. They are the words found between angle brackets and they allow tables and images among others to tell the browser what needs to be rendered on the page. HTML tags perform a variety of functions. They do not show up when you use a browser to view the page. You only see their effects. The most basic and simplest of tags do not have a lot of functions. They merely apply formatting to texts.

For example, they can make the text bold or italicized. If you want to make a text bold, you simply have to place it between <b> and </b> such as the following example:

< b > This text is bold. < /b >
This text is not bold.

As you can see in the example shown above, the first text is bold while the second one is not. The second text is not bold because it is outside of the code that makes texts bold.

9

**Does it take a long time to study HTML and learn how to write codes using it?**
It actually depends on your ability to learn a new computer language and grasp its fundamentals. If you have studied programming before and/or have had some training or experience with writing codes, you may have an advantage over first timer or newbies. Since you are already familiar with computer programming, it may not take a long time for you to transition from your previous language to HTML.

Then again, it still depends on your ability. Some first timers are fast learners. They can learn HTML in just a few days. More advanced programmers can learn the fundamentals in less than an hour. You can start creating HTML pages the moment you learn how to use tags.

If you want to create impressive websites, you have to learn about the most recent techniques as well as the correct usage of tags. You also have to learn more about graphic design and typography to further improve your skills.

**Does one have to be online all the time?**
No. You can actually write codes for your website while you are offline. You can store the files on your computer and then transfer them online later on. Each time you have a new code, you can add it to your existing program online.

**Are there things that HTML is not capable of doing?**
Yes. HTML is not perfect, but its developers are constantly finding ways to make improvements. You may also want to learn about cascading stylesheets and JavaScript for your HTML programs. The previous controls how pages are presented as well as make them more accessible while the latter adds more functionality to basic HTML.

## *Introduction to CSS*

Cascading Style Sheets, more commonly referred to as CSS, is a simple design language used to make developing websites easier. It is basically used to define the styles of Web pages, including their layout, design, variations in display for various devices, and sizes of screens.

It deals with the feel and look part of the Web page. With it, you have the power to control the styles of your fonts, colors of your texts, spacing between your paragraphs, sizes and layouts of your columns, background colors and background images of your website, designs of your overall layout, sizes of your screen, display variation in multiple devices, and a lot of other amazing effects.

The language is very easy to grasp and learn. It also gives you control over your HTML documents' presentation. More often than not, CSS is used in combination with markup languages XHTML and HTML.

CSS allows you to make the most of your available time. With this language, you only have to write your code once and reuse it over and over. You can reuse the same sheet for different HTML pages. Also, you can define a style for every HTML element and then apply it to multiple Web pages.

CSS makes pages load faster. There is no more need for you to write HTML tag attributes all the time. You can simply write one CSS rule for a tag and then apply it to the rest of its occurrences. The fewer codes there are, the faster the downloading time will be.

CSS allows for easier maintenance. If you want to make a significant change, all you have to do is change the style. The elements in your Web pages will then update automatically.

CSS has much better styles than HTML. It has more attributes too. Thus, you can make your HTML page look better as compared to when you use HTML attributes.

CSS allows content to be displayed on multiple types of devices. So, whatever electronic device you use, you can view the Web page in it. You can use the same HTML document to display different website versions on handheld devices, including cell phones and PDAs, and then print it out.

CSS is also recommended to be used instead of HTML attributes. If you want your Web pages to be compatible with future browsers, you have to use CSS in every HTML page.

With regard to offline browsing, you can rely on CSS to locally store Web applications. It can do this because of an offline cache. It allows you to check out offline websites. This cache also makes sure that the website loads faster and has a better overall performance.

Furthermore, CSS offers platform independence. It also supports the most recent browsers available.

***Frequently Asked Questions (FAQ)***

**Was CSS a solution to a particular issue or problem?**
Yes, CSS was actually a solution to a huge problem. HTML was not really meant to feature tags for Web page formatting. It was merely designed to describe its content. Consider the following examples:

```
< h1 > This is an example of a heading < /h1 >
< p > This is an example of a paragraph < /p >
```

The moment color attributes and tags became additions to HTML 3.2, Web developers experienced a lot of problems. The development of huge websites in which color and font information were included at every page became an expensive and tedious process. Because of this issue, the World Wide Web Consortium developed CSS. Its development was such a huge relief for Web developers because it got rid of the style formatting from HTML pages.

## Does CSS save a lot of work?
Yes, it does. Style definitions are typically saved in an external .css file. This external stylesheet file allows you to change the appearance of your whole website simply by changing a file.

## Who created CSS?
Håkon Wium Lie first proposed the CSS language on the 10th of October 1994. At that time, Lie was working with Tim Berners-Lee at CERN. A few other style sheet languages were also proposed for the Web. When discussions about public mailing lists were made, the first recommendation on CSS was done by the World Wide Web Consortium in 1996. The proposal of Bert Bos was particularly influential, which is why he is also considered as the co-creator of CSS.

## Who maintains CSS?
A group of individuals within the World Wide Web Consortium, known as the CSS Working Group, maintains CSS. They also create specifications, which are documents. These specifications eventually become recommendations once they were discussed and ratified officially by the members of the World Wide Web Consortium.

## Why are ratified specifications referred to as recommendations?
They are called as such due to the fact that the World Wide Web Consortium no longer has any control over the implementation of CSS. Independent organizations and companies create the software. The World Wide Web Consortium is a group of individuals that makes recommendations with regard to how the Internet needs to evolve and how it works.

# HTML Versions

## History and Versions
As you know, HTML is a continuously evolving computer language. Therefore, you cannot expect it to stay the same for a long time. A revised set of specifications and standards are created in order to adapt with the evolving needs and requirements of users.

## HTML 1.0
It was the first ever version of HTML that was released to the public. During the time of its release, however, not a lot of people were into creating websites. Thus, this version of the computer language was limiting. All a user can do back then was put some simple texts on the Internet.

## HTML 2.0
It was an improved version of HTML 1.0. It had everything its predecessor had, but with the addition of new features. It became the standard for website design in the mid-1990 because it defined a lot of core features.

## HTML 3.0
By the time it was released to the public, more people have been into programming and Web developing. More people have become familiar with HTML and wanted to use it for creating websites. Webmasters wanted more to creating websites. They wanted their websites to look attractive and inviting.

However, there came a problem. During that time, the Netscape company was leading the browser market. They offered the Netscape Navigator, which was a browser. In their desire to appease the requests and demands of HTML users, they came up with proprietary tags as well as attributes. They called these abilities the Netscape extension tags.

When the other companies learned of these tags, they tried to produce replicas that mimic the effects of such tags. However, their browsers are not able to display the same output. So, if you design a Web page using the Netscape extension tags, you will not be able to get your desired output using different browsers. You will only end up being confused and annoyed.

Then, a work group headed by Dave Raggett came up with HTML 3.0. This version of HTML was better than the two previous versions in terms of features. It had a lot of new abilities and more opportunities for users to create amazing Web page designs. Unfortunately, the browsers were slow to implement such improvements. Only a few improvements were added, mainly because of the size. Eventually, HTML 3.0 was no longer used.

Due to this failure, the developers noted that improvements have to be modular. They should be added in stages so that browser companies will not have a hard time.

## HTML 3.2
Browser specific tags continue to come. Eventually, it was apparent that there has to be a certain standard. In 1994, the World Wide Web Consortium (W3C) was founded to standardize the computer language and ensure that it keeps evolving to fit the needs and requirements of users.

The World Wide Web Consortium created HTML 3.2 and gave it a code name WILBUR. The version was a reduced change to the current standards. It was considered to be the official standard in 1997. To this date, it is still fully supported by all browsers.

## HTML 4.01
It was a huge evolution from the previous versions. It was also the final iteration of the classic HTML. During the early

stages of its development, it was given the code name COUGAR. A lot of its functionalities were derived from HTML 3.0. There were also plenty of trimmings on old tags, support for the new supporting presentational language, cascading stylesheets, and internationalism.

In December 1997, the World Wide Web Consortium recommended HTML 4.0. In April 1998, it eventually became the official standard. Microsoft undertook browser support for the Internet Explorer browser. Internet Explorer 5 and Internet Explorer 6 both offer support for nearly every tag and attribute.

## HTML 4.01
After HTML 4.0 has been released for a while, the developers made some corrections and revisions in its documentation. This resulted in HTML 4.01.

## XHTML 1.0
The World Wide Web Consortium issued the specifications for XHTML 1.0 around the start of the $21^{st}$ century as a recommendation. In January 2000, it became a joint standard with HTML 4.01.

This version represents a whole new HTML branch, which was a departure from the old ways of using specs. XHTML included rigors of XML. The code has to be written properly in order for it to work when it reaches the browser. XHTML also did not have a lot of deprecated or new attributes and tags, although certain things have changed with a view of improved functionality and accessibility. There are new sets of coding rules for users.

## HTML 5
After XHTML 1.0 and HTML 4.0 were released, the developers wanted to come up with XHTML 2. They also wanted new innovations. However, their proposal turned out

to be unrealistic and boring that the project was no longer pursued. They had to find another approach.

During this time, several fans of the pragmatic Web technology, specification writers, and browser programmers, started to create something using methods that are beyond the typical procedures used by the World Wide Web Consortium. They referred to their group as the Web Hypertext Application Technology Working Group (WHATWG). They created a new specification.

The World Wide Web Consortium eventually decided that HTML remains to be the future of the World Wide Web. HTML 5 was regarded as the new specification when XHTML 2 was discontinued. HTML 5 was specifically designed for the World Wide Web. At present, it is still used.

# CSS Versions

### *CSS 1*

This version of CSS first came out as a recommendation by the World Wide Web Consortium in December 1996. It describes the language and the simple visual formatting models of HTML tags.

### *CSS 2*

This version of CSS became a recommendation of the World Wide Web Consortium in May 1998. It was built on the previous version. It features support for style sheets that are media-specific such as aural devices, prints, element positioning, tables, and downloadable fonts.

### *CSS 3*

This version of CSS became a recommendation of the World Wide Web Consortium in June 1999. It was built on the previous versions. It features divided documentations known as modules. Every module has a new extension feature that was defined in the second version of CSS.

CSS 3 modules also have the old specifications and extension features of CSS 2. These include the box model, selectors, backgrounds, borders, replaced content, image values, text effects, animations, user interface, multiple column layout, 2D transformations, and 3D transformations.

# CHAPTER 2:
# ACCESSING THE WEB

## Going Online

### *Web Browsers*
Users can visit websites on the Internet using a web browser, which is a type of software. Some of the most commonly used web browsers are Google Chrome, Internet Explorer, Mozilla Firefox, Opera, and Safari.

If you want to view a particular web page, you have to type its address on your browser. You can also use a bookmark or follow the link that takes you to the website by clicking on it.

Manufacturers of software release a new version of their browser on a regular basis. Each time, they add a new feature as well as supporting additions to the computer language.

Then again, it is crucial for you to take note that a lot of users do not run the most recent versions of their browsers. Thus, you cannot expect everyone who visits your website to use the most recent functionalities offered by the updated browsers. You have to consider this fact when you create a website.

If you want to make sure that you can reach everyone from different parts of the world, you have to make your website compatible with the browser that they use. Aside from using the updated versions, you should also make your website viewable by users with older versions of browsers.

### *Web Servers and Devices*
The moment you ask the browser you use for a web page, it automatically sends a request across the World Wide Web.

This request is taken to a special computer called the web server. The web server hosts the websites that you see on the Internet. It stays connected online all the time. It is also optimized to cater to users who request for web pages.

There are huge companies and organizations that run their very own web servers. Nevertheless, it is still more convenient to hire a web hosting company to run your web servers. You can find paid and free hosting services. Of course, which one you will choose depends on your preference and needs.

You have to check out reviews and do the researches before you settle with a particular web hosting company. In addition, you have to keep in mind that free hosting services are usually limited. So, you will not be able to take advantage of all the features that paid versions offer.

When it comes to devices, users go to websites using their laptops, desktop computers, mobile phones, and tablets among others. Because users can now go online using a wide variety of devices, you have to make sure that your website can be displayed properly on these devices. Keep in mind that they have different sizes of screen as well as different loading times. Some devices connect faster to the Internet as compared to the others.

### Screen Readers
These are programs that scan and read the contents of a screen to the user. More often than not, they are used by individuals who have poor eyesight or some visual impairment.

You have to know that a lot of countries have certain legislations with regard to public buildings being accessible by people who have disabilities. In the same manner, websites are required by the law to be accessible to people with disabilities.

Aside from people with disabilities, screen readers are also useful to people who are jogging or driving. Because it is dangerous to keep your eyes off the road when you jog or drive, you can use a screen reader. The device allows you to do what you have to do while still knowing the content of the website that you visited.

# Search Engine Optimization (SEO)

## *The Basics of SEO*

Search engine optimization (SEO) refers to the practice of making your website appear on top of the search results. Each time a user types a certain keyword or key phrase to search for a topic, your website can pop up on the results of the search engine if it features related content.

The main idea behind search engine optimization is to find out what users are likely to type into their search engines. What terms do you think they will use to find your website? Once you find out what these terms are, you have to incorporate them into your website so that you can boost your chances of being indexed by the search engines.

Search engines determine which websites come out first at the search results by checking out the content of websites and considering how many websites are linked to them. They also consider the relevance of these links.

Search engine optimization is usually divided into two categories: off page techniques and on page techniques.

## *Off-Page Techniques*

It is important for you to get other websites to connect to you. These links contribute to your ranking. Search engines determine the ranking of your website by checking out how many other websites are linked to yours. They are interested in websites that feature relevant content.

Say, for instance, your website is an online store that sells fish bait. It would be highly irrelevant to link it to a website that features hair care and hair products. On the other hand, a website about angling would be considered relevant.

In addition, search engines check out the words found between the closing and opening tags in the links. If the texts in the links contain keywords instead of merely 'click here' and website URLs, the search engines will consider them relevant. Take note that the words on your website links also have to show up in the texts of the web pages that your website is linked to.

### *On-Page Techniques*
You can improve your ranking in the search engines by using on page techniques on your web pages. The primary idea behind these techniques is that users are likely to input certain keywords on their search engines, which is why you have to use this to your advantage and include these keywords in the HTML code and text of your website.

This way, the search engines will be informed that your website covers the topics that the keywords are pertaining to. Keep in mind that search engines largely depend on the texts in web pages. Hence, it is crucial for you to use terms that users are likely to search for. You have to put these terms in your text.

You have to make your keywords appear on the important places. Also, you have to make sure that your images contain the right texts in their alt attribute so that the search engines can easily understand their content.

Where are these important places that your keywords have to appear? In general, there are seven of them:

### 1. Page Title
It is found at the top of your browser window. It can also be found on tab of your browser. The page title is specified in the title element, which is found inside the head element.

### 2. Web Address or URL
It includes the name of your file. As much as possible, you have to use keywords or key phrases in your file name.

### 3. Headings
The search engines can find out if a page is relevant to a subject and give it more weight than the other texts if you use keywords or key phrases in your heading element.

### 4. Text
As much as possible, you have to repeat your keywords or key phrases in the main body of your text. You have to repeat them at least two to three times. Then again, you should refrain from overusing them. Otherwise, your readers may no longer understand your content. If you want visitors to keep coming back to your website, you have to make your content easy to read and understand.

### 5. Link Text
You have to use keywords or key phrases in the texts that create the links between web pages instead of generic expressions. While 'click here' is pretty straightforward on its purpose, your visitors may think that it is a clickbait or something that is not that important.

### 6. Image Alt Text
The search engines want you to give accurate descriptions of the images in your alt text. By doing so, you also make your images show up when users use images to search for results in the search engines.

### 7. Page Descriptions
Your description is found in the element. It is specified with the use of a meta tag. Keep in mind that your page descriptions have to be sentences that describe the content of your web page.

Even though they are not displayed your browser window, they may show up in the search engine results. It is never ideal to try fooling the search engines by doing certain techniques such as adding texts that are of the same colors as the backgrounds of your pages. If you do, you will get penalized and you website may get banned.

### *Identifying Keywords and Key Phrases*

If you want your website to appeal to users and search engines, you have to use the most popular and most relevant keywords and key phrases. However, this can be quite tedious if you are not very familiar with search engine optimization. Fortunately, you can determine the appropriate keywords and key phrases for your website by using the following methods:

### 1. Brainstorm

You have to make a list of all the keywords and key phrases that a user may type into a search engine. Put yourself in the shoes of an online user. In particular, you have to put yourself in the shoes of a person who may be interested in what your website is all about. Think of your target audience.

What are the services or products that you offer on your website? What are the topics or issues that you discuss? You can ask others and find out which words they are most likely to use when they want to search for your website. People who are not familiar with a certain topic may use a different term to refer to it. In other words, they may not use jargons that are specific to your industry.

Aside from keywords, you can use key phrases if your website features topics that cannot be described with just one word. A lot of users are also likely to use keywords to search for a particular topic, service, or product.

### 2. Organize

See to it that you organize your keywords and key phrases into lists. You have to group them according to section or category. This way, you can easily locate them.

For instance, if your website is an online pet store, you can group keywords for animals according to category. You can separate rabbits, dogs, and cats.

If your website is larger or you have more items to offer online customers, you can use sub-categories. This way, you can group items according to brand and model, not just type.

## 3. Research

You can use a variety of tools to help you find out more about the keywords and key phrases that online users use. When you input a keyword, the tools will give suggestions regarding other keywords that you may want to use.

For instance, you can use Google Adwords. If you use it, you have to choose 'exact match' instead of 'broad match'. You can also use Wordtracker and Keyword Discovery. After these tools provide you with keywords, you can add them to your lists. These tools are likely to suggest terms that are not relevant. You have to choose which ones are relevant for your website and discard the rest.

## 4. Compare

Your website cannot show up on top of the search results every time a user inputs a keyword. It is just not likely to appear on top all the time, especially if the topics you have on your website are common. If you have a lot of competitors, you have to make comparisons.

Keep in mind that the more websites optimize a certain keyword, the more difficult it will be for you to go up the search engines when online users type in that keyword.

There are keyword research websites that can provide you with data with regard to how many online users used for a certain keyword or key phrase. This is really helpful because you will be able to determine how much competition your terms have.

In addition, you can take advantage of the advanced search feature of Google to search for titles of pages. By doing this, you can identify the number of websites that feature your keywords in their page titles. Take note that the more pages contain the terms you use, the more competitors you have.

## 5. Refine

You have to choose which keywords and key phrases you need to concentrate on. You should always go for keywords and key phrases that are relevant to the sections of your website.

In case there is a certain phrase that is highly relevant yet has plenty of competition, you must not be hesitant to use it. In order for you to increase the odds of your website being found, you may check out if there are other terms that you can incorporate with your keywords and key phrases.

Say, for instance, if the service or information you provide on your website targets a specific location, you have to incorporate this location into the list of keywords and key phrases that you use. You have to do this so that people can find your website.

If your website promotes a certain company in a certain country, then you have to get hundreds of people from that country that are in search of products or services that this certain company offers. It would be pointless to get thousands of people who are not even in that country or are looking for a different type of product or service.

## 6. Map

Once you have created a list of keywords and key phrases, knew about your competitors, and found out about the most relevant keywords and key phrases, you have to choose which keywords and key phrases you are going to use for every web page.

You can choose three to five keywords and key phrases that map to every page of the website. Then, you can use them as your keywords and key phrases for every page.

Keep in mind that there is no more need for you to repeat them on all your pages. In addition, your keywords and key phrases can be more specific towards the individual topics you have on every page as you go farther away from your homepage towards the different sections on the website.

# Analytics

### *How many people come to your website?*

Once online visitors come to your website, you can begin to analyze how they arrived, what they were searching for, and when they are going to leave the website. Google Analytics is a very popular tool that webmasters use to figure these things out.

In order to use it, you need to sign up for an account. You just have to go to the Google website and search for analytics. You can also type in www.google.com/analytics and start from there. On the website, you will be provided with a tracking code. You need to use this tracking code on all the pages of your website.

Each time an online visitor loads your web page, your tracking code sends out data to the servers in which it is kept. Then, Google provides an interface that is web-based. You can use it to see how online users use and navigate through your website.

Google Analytics provide the tracking code, which should show up before the closing tag. The appearance of web pages is not altered by the tracking code. It does not really have any major effect on your website.

### *Where can you see how many online users come to your website?*

You can use the overview page to obtain this information. It provides you with a snapshot of the data that you are likely to search for. It particularly informs you of how many online users come to your website.

The amount of times online users come to your website is called visit. If a visitor is no longer active on your website for half an hour and then suddenly goes to another page on your website, that gets counted as a new visit.

The total amount of online users who have come to your website over a certain period of time is called unique visit. The amount of unique visits gets lower than the amount of visits if online users return to your website more than once over a certain period of time.

The total amount of pages that your online visitors view on your website is called page views. The average amount of web pages your online visitors check out on your website for every visit is known as page per visit. The average time on site refers to how much time your online users spend on your website for every visit.

If you wish to switch up the time your reports display on your website, you have to use the date selector, which is found at the upper right corner of your website. Each time you log in, you will notice that it is set to the final month of the year. Nonetheless, you can easily change it to display the date that you prefer.

If you wish to export statistics for other applications, you have to use the export link. It is found above the title that shows 'visitors overview'.

### What does your visitors look at and where do they come from?
When online users come to your website, what do you think they look at? Well, you can know more about what your visitors search for when they arrive at your website by using the content link at the left part of your website.

The pages tell you about the pages that online users are likely to look at since these pages receive the most views. It also tells you about the pages that your visitors spend a lot of time checking out.

The landing pages refer to the pages that online users get to when they first visit your website. They are very helpful since you can learn about the users that do not come to your website through your homepage.

The top exit pages tell you about the pages that online users tend to leave or exit from. If there are plenty of users who leave from a certain page, you may consider improving or changing that page.

The bounce rate refers to the amount of online users who exited on the same web page that they came to. If there is a high bounce rate on your website, there is a huge possibility that online users did not find what they were looking for on your pages. It could also be that your website is not attractive or enticing enough for your visitors to stay and look around.

A closed browser, used back button, entered new URL, clicked links to other sites, and clicked advertisements all count as a bounce.

So, where do your online visitors come from? You can check out the traffic sources link located at the left side of your website.

The referrers display the websites that connect you and the amount of visitors who came to your website through them. If a website sends huge amounts of traffic to your website, you can contact the other website and ask if you can work together as a team. This way, you can make sure that traffic continues to flow into your website. You may also search for other similar websites and request for a connection.

The direct displays which pages visitors get to if they did not arrive through another site or a link. They may have typed in your URL into their browsers, clicked on a link from an email, Word document, or PDF file, or used a bookmark on their browsers.

The search terms displays the terms that online users input into search engines to look for your website. This allows you to learn about the ways your visitors search for the content of your website. Oftentimes, the way they describe what they need is different from the way you describe your own website. Hence, you can improve your content, keywords, and key phrases.

The advanced features can be accessed through the help files of Google Analytics. If you own an online store, you should consider checking out e-commerce tracking. It adds data on the products or services you have sold, the average size of baskets, etc.

Moreover, you can create goals and specific which paths you wish your visitors would take. Then, you should see how far they would get through these paths. Knowing all these allows you to obtain as much data and information as online users as possible.

### Domain Names and Hosting

You need to have a domain name as well as web hosting if you want your website to be up and running.

The domain name refers to the web address. It is basically the URL that online users type in order to arrive at a particular website or web page.

There are a lot of websites that let you register a domain name. More often than not, you have to pay a yearly fee to keep your domain name. Do not worry, though. The fee is usually minimal.

When you choose a domain name, you will be asked to verify if your preferred name is still available. Keep in mind that since the advent of the Internet, people have started registering domain names. Thus, the domain name that you want may have already been taken by someone else. It may even take some time before you finally find a domain name that is suitable for your website.

Aside from registering a domain name, you also need to obtain web hosting. Usually, the websites that allow you to register a domain name also offers web hosting. Many of them even offer packages and discounts if you avail of both services from their website. So, if you want to save some money, you have to take advantage of this offer.

What is web hosting exactly? Web hosting is the process of giving access and storage space for websites.

In order for people to find your website, you have to upload it to a server. A web server is a special computer that is always connected online. It is designed and developed to serve web pages every time they are asked for.

A lot of websites, excluding huge websites, rely on web servers to stay up and running. These web servers are run by companies that offer web hosting services. Using a web server is more practical and economical for users who are on a budget and want to go for something reliable.

The disk space refers to the overall size of the files that consist of your website. These files include your CSS and HTML files, scripts, and images.

The bandwidth refers to how much data is sent to your visitors by the hosting company. So, how much data do you actually use? Well, for example, there are ten people who checked out all the pages of your website. This becomes the equivalent to ten times the available amount of disk space that you used.

The backups verify if the hosting company does backups on your website. It also tells you how often the hosting company does this. Take note that certain users merely create backups in order for them to be able to restore websites in case there was server breaking. The others let you access backups, which are helpful in case of emergencies, such as when you break your website accidentally as you try to keep it updated.

A lot of hosting companies provide web hosting packages to email servers. So, when it comes to email accounts, you may want to check out the size of the mailbox as well as the number of mailboxes that you are allowed to use.

If you run a content management system, you can expect it to use a database and a server side programming language. For instance, a PHP may have a MySQL database while an ASP.net may have an SQL server database. See to it that you verify with the hosting company if they support such technologies. Otherwise, you may have a problem with the software that you need to use.

Usually, it is worth looking for a review of a hosting company. By checking out reviews, you can see and find out about the experiences of other people or customers with a certain hosting company.

Sadly, you can only verify the reliability of a hosting company in the event that something goes wrong. Usually, when things are going smoothly and in order, you will not be able to detect their shortcomings. It is only when there is a problem or emergency that you can prove if they are worth your time and money.

In times of trouble or emergency situations, can the hosting company help you out? Is the hosting company going to stick with you and continue to support you? Then again, no hosting company is perfect. So, if the reviews seem too good to be true, they probably are fake. Even the best hosting companies sometimes encounter down times, and you may read about these in their negative reviews.

When it comes to hosted services, you can find numerous online services that let you point a domain name to a server. Most blogging platforms such as Tumblr, Posterous, and WordPress provide servers to their users. Likewise, e-commerce websites such as Shopify and Big Cartel provide servers on which the websites of the users are hosted on.

So, if you are on a similar platform, there is no more need for you to get a separate hosting for your website. Then again, you may still need to get a new hosting for your email.

# CHAPTER 3:
## HOW TO CREATE A WEBSITE

## Fundamentals

### *Understanding HTML and CSS*

Every Web page you see online uses HTML to format its page to be displayed in your Web browser. Whether a website is for shopping, blogging, or researching, it uses HTML. All search engines, personal websites, and entertainment websites feature HTML.

Keep in mind that hand coding your Web page using HTML is not the easiest way to make a website. Actually, it is the least efficient and slowest way to create it. Depending on the inclinations you have, it can even be the most tedious.

So, if all you desire is to have a website, you should consider using a visual Web editor instead. A visual Web editor, also commonly referred to as WYSIWYG Web editor is a computer program that allows you to design a website with little to no technical knowledge. WYSIWYG stands for What You See Is What You Get. Basically, whatever you see is really what you get.

Also, HTML alone will not do the job. If you expect to achieve the output that professional Web designers produce, you have to use other tools. You cannot rely on HTML for all the features and functions that you want.

For instance, HTML does not suffice when you want to have at least two columns on your website, if you want to change colors or use a variety of font types, or if you want to perform other visual design tasks to make the Web page look more attractive and presentable.

This is where CSS comes in. CSS is the technology that HTML needs. You have to use it to control the appearance of the website. Your website will not be complete unless you use CSS after HTML. Both of them have to work with each other.

The entire process seems complicated, especially to individuals who do not know much or anything at all about programming and Web developing. If you want to have it easier, you should probably just use a visual Web editor that instantaneously creates the HTML and CSS codes for you.

### Beginning HTML and CSS

If you are ready to begin HTML and CSS, you need to get a text editor. You can choose from a wide variety of HTML editors. A good HTML editor provides you with a built-in browser window, which you can use to preview your Web page.

A good HTML editor also features a validator, which you can use to look for any mistakes that you have made. It is as if you are using a spell checker in the word process. Then again, no spell check is perfect. Even the best one cannot identify every mistake present in the file. The same thing goes with a validator.

Thus, you have to be good at identifying errors on your own. You need to have a sharp eye to catch mistakes and typographical errors. If you do not have the skills for this but you want your work to be flawless, you can hire a writer and an editor. Take note that the entire Web page can suffer if you miss even just one closing tag.

You have to be very careful when you type your code. As much as possible, you have to type slowly. However, if you think that typing slowly wastes a lot of time, you can just hire someone else to check your work for you. Your work has to be checked for mistakes and typographical errors, as well as tested for functionality.

When searching for an HTML editor on the Internet, you may find some services or websites that offer pre-designed templates. While these templates are convenient and easy to use, they prevent you from producing a unique output.

You can use a pre-designed template to make a website, but it will not be one of a kind. It will function the same way as other websites that also used the same kind of pre-designed template. Hence, it is much better to design your own website yourself.

In addition, you have to keep in mind that using a Notepad is not ideal. Some people use Notepad for their HTML and CSS codes. Notepad is a program that comes with Windows computers. However, a Notepad is not exactly a proper text editor.

If you have to code directly using HTML, you need to use a fully functional text editor. There are free and paid versions of text editors. If you merely use Notepad, it will not be able to handle all the characters and character combinations that you use.

If you insist on using the Notepad, then you also have to limit the characters and character combinations that you use on your code. Otherwise, your file may end up being corrupted. Worse, you will not be notified of this. There are no error messages or warnings.

What's more, Notepad does not have the capacity to deal with huge files. Hence, there is a tendency for it to invoke another program such as Wordpad. When this happens, things can get much worse for you because Wordpad will most certainly corrupt the Web page.

Even developers from Microsoft do not recommend using Notepad as a text editor. Notepad was created for regular computer users for the casual viewing of log files and other things. It was not intended to do programming work.

Aside from the Notepad, you also have to refrain from using a word processor to deal with your HTML codes. Word processors actually insert invisible and hidden codes that are not part of HTML into files.

What are these word processors? These include any program that lets you create tables, underline texts, and do other things on a word file. Microsoft Office, Open Office, and Libre Office are all subject to this. Since Wordpad is basically a word processor, you should refrain from using it for such purpose.

If you are on a budget, are just starting out as a Web developer, or want to test a text editor first, you can try free versions such as BlueGriffon and KompoZer. They are open source Web editors that you can download for free. KompoZer, however, may no longer be suitable for modern Web standards due to its outdated support.

How about if you have Dreamweaver? If you have this on your computer, then there is no more need for you to obtain a separate text editor. You can simply switch to the code view by clicking on View from your menu bar and then Code from the drop down menu. Dreamweaver will then switch from the visual design interface to the text editor interface.

Dreamweaver features a built-in text editor that is ideal for individuals who write codes using HTML. In addition, it features tools that allow you to check your codes and correct them. You can also switch to Design view if you want to see a preview of your Web page on a browser. Furthermore, Dreamweaver allows you to publish Web pages using its site synchronization facilities.

# Getting Started with HTML

## *Your Very First Web Page*

Everything has a first time. Just like everything that you do for the first time, creating a web page can both be exciting and nerve-wracking. You are excited because you can finally do something on your own. You can create a website from scratch and test out the efficiency of your codes. At the same time, you are also nervous because you are afraid that your code will not work or your computer will be damaged.

Then again, if you do not take the leap, you will forever be stuck. You will also regret not having the courage to just do it. So, with this being said, you should begin creating a website right now.

```
<!DOCTYPE HTML PUBLIC " - // W3C // DTD HTML 4.01
Transitional // EN."
"http : // www.sampleprogram.com / TR / html4 / loose.dtd " >
< html >
< head >
< /head >
< body >
< p >
This is a sample web page that is not involved with any website.
< /p >
< /body >
< /html >
```

Take note that the above given example is not actually connected to any website. www.sampleprogram.com is non-existent. This example is given as a mere guide for you to know how you should write your code.

Anyway, you can start with this sample HTML page. You have to put it into the text editor and then save it with a file name of "sample.html". You have to save it on your desktop.

You may think that this step is not necessary, but it actually is. This simple step helps you learn more about creating websites using HTML codes. As you go through the learning process, you also learn how to modify codes to improve your program. In addition, you become more familiar with your text editor. Soon enough, you will be comfortable using it.

The text you input into your text editor may vary in color, depending on the text editor that you use. Different text editors have different colors. You should not worry about this. These colors are what webmasters and programmers refer to as syntax highlighting. You can simply ignore it since it does not have any major effect on your program anyway.

To save your file, you just have to click on File from the menu and then click on Save from the sub-menu. When you are prompted to enter a filename, you have to choose the right folder in order for your file to be saved. In this case, you have to save your file on your desktop so that you can easily and quickly see it for future use and reference. Type in "sample.html".

You have learned from a previous chapter that Notepad is not a recommended text editor. So, you should not use Notepad for this code. If you use Notepad, it will only change the filename into "sample.html.txt" and you will not get the output that you want.

 Even though you can rename it, it is still much better to use a proper text editor. This is especially true if you are dealing with huge files. As you have learned, Notepad may call on Wordpad, which can cause problems with your program.

When you are done saving the file, you have to open this file in your browser. You can simply double click on it and then you should see it show up on your default browser. You have to keep both your text editor and browser open. Refrain from exiting or closing any of the programs.

### HTML Logic

Check out your HTML code. You can view it on your text editor. Read the text that is shown on your browser. Still using the same example given above, the words say "This is a sample web page that is not involved with any website." As you can see, the sentence is positioned between the tags <p> and the </p>. The whole block is positioned between the tags <body> and </body>.

If you look at the code closely, you will realize that there are other words that are within angle brackets such as <head> and </head> as well as <html> and </html>. The words that are found within these angle brackets are referred to as HTML tags.

Most of the tags in HTML come in pairs. The <body>, for instance, is used to signify the beginning of a sentence while the slash ( / ) is used to signify the end of a sentence. So, when you see </body>, you can expect to find a sentence that was ended.

Keep in mind that every tag represents a particular function. For instance, the tags <p> and </p> are used to signify the beginning and end of a particular paragraph.

### HTML Documents

To help you learn about web page structures faster, you should think of a regular business letter. How does this letter look like? What are its parts or components?

In general, a business letter is a formal letter that needs to follow a specific format. It has to include a letterhead or the address of the sender, as well as the address of the receiver. It also has to include the name of the receiver, followed by the main content of the letter.

Just like business letters, web pages need to follow a specific format too.

First of all, your first line has to identify the version and type of the HTML that you use for your web page. Then, you have to enclose the rest of your web page with the tags <html> and </html>. You have to enclose your codes between these tags in order to form your web page.

The first part of your web page is referred to as the HEAD section. In this section, the tag <head> starts it while the tag </head> ends it. It is where information that is meant for the search engines and web browsers are found. Take note that the codes you put in this section of your web page are not yet shown in the web browser.

You can compare this with the address that you put at the start of your business letter. Such address serves a purpose, even if it is not exactly part of your main content. Still using the sample code given above, you can see that the HEAD section is empty. Since you are a beginner, you may be confused if there are too many words included in the example. As you learn how to write codes, you will know how to write the correct HEAD section.

Then, there is the BODY section. It is where the information shown in the web browser is located. It is enclosed with the tags <body> and </body>.

### DOCTYPE or DTD
Still referring to the above given example, you can see the words

```
< ! DOCTYPE HTML PUBLIC " - // W3C // DTD HTML 4.01
Transitional // EN "
" http : // www.sampleprogram.com / TR / html4 / loose.dtd " >
```

So, what does this mean exactly? Well, unlike other lines on the web page, it is not an HTML tag. It is actually a version identifier that informs web browsers about the HTML version that you use on your web page. Many of the websites

43

you see on the Internet today use HTML 4.01 and XHTML 1.0. As you have learned from a previous chapter, these versions are practically similar.

It is just that XHTML is much more sensitive towards certain things such as the use of uppercase and lowercase letters on the words you use for tags. It is also sensitive with regard to using closing tags.

As a beginner, it is recommended that you choose HTML 4.01 over XHTML 1.0. The latter does not really do much for your website than the previous. You can be fine with just HTML. So, there is really not urgent need for you to transition to XHTML.

Anyway, the version line is referred to as the DOCTYPE. It is seen at the start of the line. It is actually short for Document Type Definition. If you would like to shorten it further, you can use DTD. You will get the same results.

The Document Type Definition does a lot for your web browser. Aside from providing information on the HTML version that you use, it also tells if your web page uses a type of HTML technology known as frames, if it is a normal web page, or if it is a normal web page that makes use of a limited HTML subset.

### The HEAD Section
You have read about the HEAD section and now have an idea on what it is about. The TITLE tag of the web page is among the most essential components of this section. It is the tag that gives search engines and web browsers information about the title of your web page. Whatever title you use for this tag does not show up on the web page. Instead, it is shown on the title bar of the browser window whenever it shows the page.

Then, you can go to the text editor and input this line on the HEAD section:

< title > This is my very first web page </title >

You have to move the cursor towards the end part of the line that contains the tag <head>. Afterwards, you have to press Enter in order to produce a line beneath it. When you are done with this, you can type in the words that you see in the above given example. See to it that you put the words between the tags <title> and </title>.

You can now save the page and refresh or reload it on your browser. You can simply press the keys Ctrl + S and Ctrl + R. When it has been saved and reloaded, you can check out the title bar on your browser window. What do you see on it? Well, you should see that the title you used has been displayed.

As you can see, the words that you entered do not show up in the main body of the web page. This is because the tag <title> merely creates the title of the web page for search engines and web browsers alone. It will not change the appearance of your web page. If you wish to display anything in particular on your web page, you have to use the BODY section.

You should take note that the TITLE tag is very important. In fact, it is a required part for all web pages. In other words, you cannot create your web page without a title tag. You should never leave that out.

### The BODY Section
In this section, you will be using the paragraph tags <p> and </p>. The tag <p> indicates that the browser has to display whatever follows it until it reaches the tag </p>.

Still using your text editor and the sample program shown

above, you have to place the text cursor at the end of the sentence:

This is a sample web page that is not involved with any website.

All you have to do is move the cursor until it reaches the period or end part of the line. Then, you have to press Enter to create a new line on your text editor. When you are done with this, you can type another sentence on the blank line. You can type anything such as the following:

The website www.sample.com is an ideal source of information for webmasters and programmers.

Then, you have to save your page and reload it on the browser just like what you did before. Check out the placement of the new sentence that you just typed. As you can see, even though you placed it on a new line on your text editor, the browser still showed it right after your first sentence. Because of this, it appears that both sentences are part of a single paragraph.

Go back to the text editor and place the cursor between any two words from your sample sentence. You can see that there is a single space between them. You can add more spaces when you hit the space bar a few times. You can add as many spaces as you want before saving the page and reloading it on your browser once more.

Check out the paragraph on the browser. As you can see, the paragraph still looks exactly the same. There were no changes at all. It is as if the browser simply swallowed the additional spaces that you put.

The new line and space characters that your text editor places on your web page when you press Enter are known as whitespaces. If you use multiple whitespaces, they will simply be replaced by one whitespace in the browser.

If you are using HTML, adding new lines or spaces to format your web page does not work. Your browser will merely ignore these additional lines and spaces. So, if you wish to format your web page, you can use additional HTML tags or CSS.

In order for you to add a new paragraph to your page, you simply have to bring the cursor towards the end of the tag </p> and then press Enter. You can now insert a new line such as the following:

< p > This example shows a new paragraph that involves the use of paragraph tags. </p>

Of course, you have to save your page once again and reload it on the browser. You should now see your newest paragraph on your page.

There is no need for you to put the tag <p> on a new line. You can just type in your new sentence right after your tag. You will get the same output even if you do not place the tag on another line. It does not really matter if you use a whitespace between your text and paragraph tag.

As a beginner, you can practice and keep doing this until you get more comfortable doing it. You have to familiarize yourself with the way browsers interpret paragraph tags and whitespaces. You can input new sentences or paragraphs to the existing paragraph tags or put the tags and sentences on one line. Reload your web page on your browser and observe the effects that you created.

# Getting Started with CSS

CSS lets you define your page style and layout in a single location, so you can apply them globally to .htm files. In the event that you have a change of heart, you can easily make changes on your file. CSS will update your .htm files in an instant. This is great because you are able to save energy and time.

If you want to add some style to a tag that you created, you can type the following:

H1 { text-align : left ; color : black ; font : normal 40pt "Times New Roman" }

By typing this, you are defining a style for the tag <h1>. <H1> is the one that describes which tag you wish you define. When you write your code, you use curly brackets or braces ( { } ) instead of angled brackets.

Text-align defines the alignment of your text. You have the option to use left-align, right-align, or center. Color refers to the color of the font you use. You can either use hex numbers or words to describe the color that you want to feature. Font is where you assign the type and size of your font. After every attribute, you have to use a semi-colon ( ; ) to separate the sections.

Since you are done defining this style, you can now connect the CSS with the .htm file. You have to save your file using a .css extension inside the CSS folder. Here is an example:

HelloCSSWorld.css

Then, you have to open the file and type the following:

< link rel = stylesheet type = "text / css" href = "css / HelloCSSWorld.css" >

When you type this, you connect the CSS file with the .htm file. Every time you create a .htm file, you have to include this tag.

After the modifications that you have done, you should have an HTML that looks similar to the following:

```
< ! DOCTYPE HTML PUBLIC "- // W3C // DTD HTML 4.01
Transitional // EN" >
< html >
< head >
< title > Hello CSS World < /title >
< link rel = stylesheet type = "text / css" href = "css /
Hellocssworld.css" >
< /head >
< body >
< h1 > Hello CSS World, a first HTML example < /h1 >
</body >
< /html >
```

# CHAPTER 4:
# HTML STRUCTURE

## Structuring Web Pages and Documents

### *How Web Pages Use Structure*

To help you understand the way web pages use structure as a beginner, you can think of a typical newspaper. How does it look like? What are its parts and features?

For every page of the newspaper, you will see a headline. It is usually followed by images and texts. Then, you will see the main article, which may include subheadings or is divided into several sub-sections. This particular structure of the newspaper allows readers to understand the article or the news report better. The page is organized and classified into their appropriate categories to prevent confusion and misinformation.

A computer program has the same concept. It needs to have a structure in order for it to run and be understood properly. If its elements are not appropriately organized, the programmer may be confused.

The following are the primary elements of HTML:

- Header
- Main
- Navigational menu
- Article
- Section
- Aside
- Address
- Footer

These elements are pretty self-explanatory. So, it should not be difficult for you to know what they are meant for, even if you are only a beginner.

## Header

This element is used for the purpose of identifying and containing the contents that shows at the beginning of each web page. These contents include the logo or branding, search bar, tagline, navigation items, and other things that are duplicated across your web pages.

More often than not, the header is placed before the body, but it can also precede the main element.

## Main

This element is found between the header and the footer, and is meant to denote the contents of your web page that are related to the primary topic or the body of your web page. It has to contain contents that are unique to this page. It should not contain contents that are duplicated across your web pages, such as navigation items, headers, and footers.

Then again, you can have more than one main element on your web page. This is especially ideal if your homepage features your most recent posts. You can have a main element for each of these posts.

## Navigational Menu

This element is usually placed at the upper part of the web page. It can also be placed in the footer or at the sidebar. You have to use the tag <nav> when using a navigational menu on your web page. Then again, there is no need for you to use this tag for all your links. Nevertheless, they are crucial for the blocks of links that navigate to a specific part or the entire website.

## Article

This element can be placed anywhere on your web page, although it is most commonly found after the main or section elements. It is ideal to be used if you have articles, blog posts, and any other contents that are syndicated.

## Section

This element is used for the purpose of determining the contents that are major sub-sections of the entire website. For instance, if you have an e-book on your web page that is in an HTML format, you can use this element for every chapter of the e-book.

Similarly, if your sidebar has several sections for the search bar, ads, signup form, and related posts, you can use the section tags for each one of these sections.

Some users are confused with using div and section. Ideally, you have to use div if you simply want your content to be easier to organize or you are using JavaScript. On the other hand, you have to use section if you want your contents to be listed as items when you write the outline of your document.

## Aside

This element can be used if your web page shows information that is related to your main content, but does not exactly constitute it. Related links and content, advertisements, and author information are usually found within this element.

For instance, if your post contains technical terms and their definitions are found on the sidebar, you should probably put these definitions in tags. This way, it would be much easier for your visitors and readers to see them. You may also want to use the tag <aside> for your sidebar in order to make it clear to your visitors that it is not a primary part of your web page.

## Address

This element is used to provide the contact information of the author or owner of the website, an article, or a document on the web page. If it is found within the body, it shows the contact information of the document. If it is found within the article, it shows the contact information for that particular article.

## Footer

This element represents a footer for the nearest sectioning root or sectioning content element. It usually contains information regarding the author, links of documents, and copyright.

## *Related Elements and Declaration*

The following are other elements that you may find in an HTML program:

## Meta

This element is used to provide additional information to the HTML document. The information that is enclosed within the tag <meta> is not shown on the website. However, it is read by web crawlers and browsers.

## Base

This element is used to determine a base URL upon which you can build all the relative URLs that you use on your web page. If it contains a target attribute, this attribute would be used as a default attribute for every hyperlink that appears on the document.

## Div

This element is used to define arbitrary blocks of content that can be placed and styled as single units.

## DOCTYPE

This declaration is used to inform the browsers of visitors that the document is an HTML document. All HTML documents have to have this declaration in order to be compliant with the HTML standards.

# CHAPTER 5:
# HTML TEXT

## Markup

When you create a web page, you have to add tags, which are referred to as markups to the content of your page. They give additional information as well as allow the browsers to display the correct structure of the page.

In general, there are two types of markups: structural and semantic. Structural markup refers to the elements that you use to identify the paragraphs and the headings. Semantic markup, on the other hand, provides addition information, such as meanings of acronyms, quoted sentences, and emphasis on sentences among others.

### *Headings*
In essence, there are six levels of headings used in HTML.

```
< h1 >
< h2 >
< h3 >
< h4 >
< h5 >
< h6 >
```

The first heading <h1> is meant for the main heading. The second heading <h2> is meant for the subheading. If you have more sections under your subheading, you have to use the third heading <h3>, the fourth heading <h4>, and so on.

Web browsers usually show the contents of headings in various sizes. For instance, the contents of the first heading <h1> have the largest size while the contents of the sixth heading <h6> have the smallest size. Then again, the sizes displayed on web browsers can vary. As a user, you have control over what size you want your texts to appear on your browser. You also have control over their color and font style.

Take a look at the following example:

```
< h1 > This is an example of the main heading < /h1 >
< h2 > This is an example of the level 2 heading < /h2 >
< h3 > This is an example of the level 3 heading < /h3 >
< h4 > This is an example of the level 4 heading < /h4 >
< h5 > This is an example of the level 5 heading < /h5 >
< h6 > This is an example of the level 6 heading < /h6 >
```

The output of the above given example should look like the following:

# This is an example of the main heading
## This is an example of the level 2 heading
### This is an example of the level 3 heading
#### This is an example of the level 4 heading
##### This is an example of the level 5 heading
###### This is an example of the level 6 heading

As you can see in the output, the sizes of the headings are different. The first heading is the largest while the sixth heading is the smallest.

### Bold and Italic
You can make your texts appear more presentable by bolding or italicizing them. These styles also make your content more readable. You can highlight or put more emphasis on words that are bolded or italicized.

If you wish to make a text bold, you have to place it between the tags <b> and </b>. These tags also represent the section that you want to display in a particular way. For instance, you can make your keywords and key phrases bold.

Consider the following example:

< p > In this example, you can see that this word is < b > bold. </b> </p>
< p > In this other example, you can see that this particular < b> keyword </b > is in bold letters. </p>

The output of the above given example should look like this:
In this example, you can see that this word is **bold.**
In this other example, you can see that this particular **keyword** is in bold letters.

As you can see in the output, only the words that were enclosed in the tags <b> and </b> were bolded. The rest of the sentence was not affected.

In the same way, an italicized word can make it stand out from the rest of the sentence. You can make a particular character italic by enclosing it in the tags <i> and </i>. Likewise, this element represents the section of your text that you want to present in a particular manner. For instance, you can italicize technical terms, quotes, foreign words, or proper names among others.

To help you understand this concept further, take a look at the following example:

< p > In this example, you can see that this word appears < i > italic. </i > </p >
< p > In this other example, you can see that this certain < i > keyword < /i > has been italicized. < /p >

The output of the above given example should look like this:

In this example, you can see that this word appears *italic.*

In this other example, you can see that this certain *keyword* has been italicized.

Just like with bold, only the words that are enclosed within the tags <i> and </i> are italicized. The rest of the sentence remains unaffected.

### *Superscript and Subscript*
If you need to include certain terms or formula in your content, you can use superscript and subscript.

The element <sup> is used to turn a character into a superscript. For example, you can use this element for mathematical concepts or dates.

Consider the following examples:

< p > We will celebrate Christmas on the 25 < sup > th < /sup > of December. < /p >

The output of the above given example should look like this:

We will celebrate Christmas on the $25^{th}$ of December.

On the other hand, the element <sub> is used to turn a character into a subscript. For example, you can use this element for chemical formulas or footnotes.

Consider the following examples:

< p > The chemical formula for water is H < sub > 2 < /sub > O. < /p >

The output of the above given example should look like this:

The chemical formula for water is $H_2O$.

# Whitespaces

You have read about whitespaces from a previous chapter. In this part of this book, you will learn more about it. First of all, a whitespace or an extra space is used by webmasters or programmers to add an extra space to a line or start a new element.

When your browser sees two spaces or more that are next to each other, it will merely display a single space. Likewise, if it sees a line break, it merely considers it a single space. This is referred to as white space collapsing.

Webmasters and programmers generally take advantage of this when indenting their code and making it easier to read. It is just more organized to see a program that is not cluttered with sentences. You can use as many spaces as necessary between the words, or even press Enter to go to a new line, and your output will stay the same.

Take a look at the following example:

< p > The girl that has no name slayed the sons of Walder Frey and fed them to him. < /p >

< p > The girl that has no name slayed the sons of Walder Frey and fed them to him.< /p >

< p > The girl that has no name slayed the sons of Walder Frey and fed them to him. < /p >

The output of the above given example should look like this:

The girl that has no name slayed the sons of Walder Frey and fed them to him.

The girl that has no name slayed the sons of Walder Frey and fed them to him.

The girl that has no name slayed the sons of Walder Frey and fed them to him.

As you can see, the output remains the same in spite of the number of spaces and line breaks used on the sentence.

# CHAPTER 6: HTML LISTS

In general, there are three ways on how you can specify your list of information. Keep in mind that every list has to contain at least one element.

A list can contain the following:

< ol > You use it for ordered lists because it makes use of various schemes in order to list the items.

< ul > - You use it for unordered lists because it lists the items with the use of bullets.

< dl > You use it for definition lists because it organizes the items as if they were in a dictionary.

## Ordered Lists

If you want to display your items with numbers rather than bullets, you have to use an ordered list. You have to use the tag <ol>. When you do, you will notice that the numbering begins at 1 and has an increment of 1 for every succeeding element. These succeeding elements, however, must be given the tag <li>.

To help you understand this concept further, you should take a look at the following example:

```
< ! DOCTYPE html >
< html >
< head >
< title > This sample program shows you how a basic
ordered list looks like < /title >
< /head >
< /body >
< ol >
```

```
< li > Colt Python < /li >
< li > Desert Eagle < /li >
< li > Diamondback < /li >
< li > Glock < /li >
< li > Grendel </li >
< li > Mauser Model < /li >
< li > Pocket Pistols < /li >
< li > Ruger Old Army Revolvers < /li >
< li > Smith and Wesson < /li >
< li > Weatherby Vanguard < /li >
< /ol >
< /body >
< /html >
```

The output of the above given example should be as follows:

1. Colt Python
2. Desert Eagle
3. Diamondback
4. Glock
5. Grendel
6. Mauser Model
7. Pocket Pistols
8. Ruger Old Army Revolvers
9. Smith and Wesson
10. Weatherby Vanguard

**The Type Attribute**

As the programmer, you are free to use the type attribute for the tag < ol > if you want. Its purpose is for specifying which type of list marker you prefer. If you do not specify a particular type, you would get a number by default, just like what you got using the sample program shown above.

The following are the type attributes you can use for ordered lists:

| Type | Description |
|---|---|
| Type = " 1 " | If you use this type, your list items would be organized by numbers. (*Default-case numerals*) |
| Type = " a " | If you use this type, your list items would be organized by lowercase letters. (*Lower-case letters*) |
| Type = " A " | If you use this type, your list items would be organized by uppercase letters. (*Upper-case letters*) |
| Type = " i " | If you use this type, your list items would be organized by lowercase Roman numerals. (*Lower-case numerals*) |
| Type = " I " | If you use this type, your list items would be organized by uppercase Roman numerals. (*Upper-case numerals*) |

To help you understand the functions of the list attributes for ordered lists, you should take a look at the following examples:

In this sample program, the type = " 1 " attribute is used:

```
< ! DOCTYPE html >
< html >
< head >
< title > This sample program shows you how an ordered list
using type 1 looks like < /title >
< /head >
< /body >
< ol type = " 1 " >
< li > Tyrion Lannister < /li >
< li > Daenerys Targaryen < /li >
< li > Arya Stark < /li >
< li > Jon Snow < /li >
< li > Sansa Stark </li >
< li > Cersei Lannister < /li >
```

```
< li > Joffrey Baratheon < /li >
< li > Jaime Lannister < /li >
< li > Brienne of Tarth < /li >
< li > Margaery Tyrell < /li >
< /ol >
< /body >
< /html >
```

The output of the above given example should be as follows:

1. Tyrion Lannister
2. Daenerys Targaryen
3. Arya Stark
4. Jon Snow
5. Sansa Stark
6. Cersei Lannister
7. Joffrey Baratheon
8. Jaime Lannister
9. Brienne of Tarth
10. Margaery Tyrell

In this sample program, the type = " a " attribute is used:

```
< ! DOCTYPE html >
< html >
< head >
< title > This sample program shows you how an ordered list
using type a looks like < /title >
< /head >
< /body >
< ol type = " a " >
< li > Zeus < /li >
< li > Hera < /li >
< li > Poseidon < /li >
< li > Aphrodite < /li >
< li > Hades </li >
< li > Demeter < /li >
```

```
< li > Apollo < /li >
< li > Athena < /li >
< li > Artemis < /li >
< li > Hermes < /li >
< /ol >
< /body >
< /html >
```

The output of the above given example should be as follows:

a. Zeus
b. Hera
c. Poseidon
d. Aphrodite
e. Hades
f. Demeter
g. Apollo
h. Athena
i. Artemis
j. Hermes

In this sample program, the type = " A " attribute is used:

```
< ! DOCTYPE html >
< html >
< head >
< title > This sample program shows you how an ordered list
using type A looks like < /title >
< /head >
< /body >
< ol type = " A " >
< li > Jupiter < /li >
< li > Juno < /li >
< li > Neptune < /li >
< li > Venus < /li >
< li > Pluto </li >
< li > Ceres < /li >
```

```
< li > Apollo < /li >
< li > Minerva < /li >
< li > Diana < /li >
< li > Mercury < /li >
< /ol >
< /body >
< /html >
```

The output of the above given example should be as follows:

A. Jupiter
B. Juno
C. Neptune
D. Venus
E. Pluto
F. Ceres
G. Apollo
H. Minerva
I. Diana
J. Mercury

In this sample program, the type = " i " attribute is used:

```
< ! DOCTYPE html >
< html >
< head >
< title > This sample program shows you how an ordered list
using type i looks like < /title >
< /head >
< /body >
< ol type = " i " >
< li > Toyota Camry < /li >
< li > Subaru Forester < /li >
< li > Lexus RX < /li >
< li > Chevrolet Impala < /li >
< li > Honda Civic </li >
< li > Subaru Outback < /li >
```

```
< li > Jeep Grand Cherokee < /li >
< li > Honda Pilot < /li >
< li > Nissan Rogue < /li >
< li > Hyundai Tucson < /li >
< /ol >
< /body >
< /html >
```

The output of the above given example should be as follows:

i. Toyota Camry
ii. Subaru Forester
iii. Lexus RX
iv. Chevrolet Impala
v. Honda Civic
vi. Subaru Outback
vii. Jeep Grand Cherokee
viii. Honda Pilot
ix. Nissan Rogue
x. Hyundai Tucson

In this sample program, the type = " I " attribute is used:

```
< ! DOCTYPE html >
< html >
< head >
< title > This sample program shows you how an ordered list
using type I looks like < /title >
< /head >
< /body >
< ol type = " I " >
< li > Toyota Camry < /li >
< li > Subaru Forester < /li >
< li > Lexus RX < /li >
< li > Chevrolet Impala < /li >
< li > Honda Civic </li >
< li > Subaru Outback < /li >
```

```
< li > Jeep Grand Cherokee < /li >
< li > Honda Pilot < /li >
< li > Nissan Rogue < /li >
< li > Hyundai Tucson < /li >
< /ol >
< /body >
< /html >
```

The output of the above given example should be as follows:

I. Toyota Camry
II. Subaru Forester
III. Lexus RX
IV. Chevrolet Impala
V. Honda Civic
VI. Subaru Outback
VII. Jeep Grand Cherokee
VIII. Honda Pilot
IX. Nissan Rogue
X. Hyundai Tucson

**The Start Attribute**

As the programmer, you are free to use the start attribute with the tag < ol > if you want. Its purpose is for specifying the beginning point of the list marker that you prefer.

This table shows you the start attributes that you can use for ordered lists. Take note that the starting point could be anywhere. You can start with whatever number you want. In the following sample table, the starting point would be number 3.

| Type Start | Description |
| --- | --- |
| Type = " 1 "  Start = " 3 " | *Numerals start with 3.* If you use this type, your list items would be organized by numbers, starting from the nominal number 3. |
| Type = " A "  Start = " 3 " | *Letters start with C.* If you use this type, your list items would be organized by uppercase letters, starting from the uppercase letter C because it is the third letter of the alphabet. |
| Type = " a "  Start = " 3 " | *Letters start with c.* If you use this type, your list items would be organized by lowercase letters, starting from the lowercase letter c because it is the third letter of the alphabet. |
| Type = " i "  Start = " 3 " | *Numerals start with iii.* If you use this type, your list items would be organized by lowercase Roman numerals, starting with the Roman numeral iii. |
| Type = " I "  Start = " 3 " | *Numerals start with III.* If you use this type, your list items would be organized by uppercase Roman numerals, starting with the Roman numeral III. |

To help you understand the functions of the list attributes for ordered lists, you should take a look at the following examples:

In this sample program, type = " 1 " start = " 3 "is used:

```
< ! DOCTYPE html >
< html >
< head >
< title > This sample program shows you how an ordered list
using type 1 start 3 looks like < /title >
< /head >
< /body >
```

68

```
< ol type = " 1 "  start = " 3 " >
< li > Tyrion Lannister < /li >
< li > Daenerys Targaryen < /li >
< li > Arya Stark < /li >
< li > Jon Snow < /li >
< li > Sansa Stark </li >
< li > Cersei Lannister < /li >
< li > Joffrey Baratheon < /li >
< li > Jaime Lannister < /li >
< li > Brienne of Tarth < /li >
< li > Margaery Tyrell < /li >
< /ol >
< /body >
< /html >
```

The output of the above given example should be as follows:

3. Tyrion Lannister
4. Daenerys Targaryen
5. Arya Stark
6. Jon Snow
7. Sansa Stark
8. Cersei Lannister
9. Joffrey Baratheon
10. Jaime Lannister
11. Brienne of Tarth
12. Margaery Tyrell

In this sample program, type = " a " start = " 3 " is used:

```
< ! DOCTYPE html >
< html >
< head >
< title > This sample program shows you how an ordered list
using type a start 3 looks like < /title >
< /head >
< /body >
```

```
< ol type = " a "  start = " 3 " >
< li > Zeus < /li >
< li > Hera < /li >
< li > Poseidon < /li >
< li > Aphrodite < /li >
< li > Hades </li >
< li > Demeter < /li >
< li > Apollo < /li >
< li > Athena < /li >
< li > Artemis < /li >
< li > Hermes < /li >
< /ol >
< /body >
< /html >
```

The output of the above given example should be as follows:

```
c. Zeus
d. Hera
e. Poseidon
f. Aphrodite
g. Hades
h. Demeter
i. Apollo
j. Athena
k. Artemis
l. Hermes
```

In this sample program, type = " A " start = " 3 "  is used:

```
< ! DOCTYPE html >
< html >
< head >
< title > This sample program shows you how an ordered list
using type A start 3 looks like < /title >
< /head >
< /body >
```

70

```
< ol type = " A " start = " 3 " >
< li > Jupiter < /li >
< li > Juno < /li >
< li > Neptune < /li >
< li > Venus < /li >
< li > Pluto </li >
< li > Ceres < /li >
< li > Apollo < /li >
< li > Minerva < /li >
< li > Diana < /li >
< li > Mercury < /li >
< /ol >
< /body >
< /html >
```

The output of the above given example should be as follows:

C. Jupiter
D. Juno
E. Neptune
F. Venus
G. Pluto
H. Ceres
I. Apollo
J. Minerva
K. Diana
L. Mercury

In this sample program, type = " i " start = " 3 " is used:

```
< ! DOCTYPE html >
< html >
< head >
< title > This sample program shows you how an ordered list
using type i start 3 looks like < /title >
< /head >
< /body >
```

```
< ol type = " i " start = " 3 " >
< li > Toyota Camry < /li >
< li > Subaru Forester < /li >
< li > Lexus RX < /li >
< li > Chevrolet Impala < /li >
< li > Honda Civic </li >
< li > Subaru Outback < /li >
< li > Jeep Grand Cherokee < /li >
< li > Honda Pilot < /li >
< li > Nissan Rogue < /li >
< li > Hyundai Tucson < /li >
< /ol >
< /body >
< /html >
```

The output of the above given example should be as follows:

```
iii. Toyota Camry
iv. Subaru Forester
v. Lexus RX
vi. Chevrolet Impala
vii. Honda Civic
viii. Subaru Outback
ix. Jeep Grand Cherokee
x. Honda Pilot
xi. Nissan Rogue
xii. Hyundai Tucson
```

In this sample program, type = " I " start = " 3 " is used:

```
< ! DOCTYPE html >
< html >
< head >
< title > This sample program shows you how an ordered list
using type I start 3 looks like < /title >
< /head >
< /body >
```

```
< ol type = " I "  start = " 3 " >
< li > Toyota Camry < /li >
< li > Subaru Forester < /li >
< li > Lexus RX < /li >
< li > Chevrolet Impala < /li >
< li > Honda Civic </li >
< li > Subaru Outback < /li >
< li > Jeep Grand Cherokee < /li >
< li > Honda Pilot < /li >
< li > Nissan Rogue < /li >
< li > Hyundai Tucson < /li >
< /ol >
< /body >
< /html >
```

The output of the above given example should be as follows:

III. Toyota Camry
IV. Subaru Forester
V. Lexus RX
VI. Chevrolet Impala
VII. Honda Civic
VIII. Subaru Outback
IX. Jeep Grand Cherokee
X. Honda Pilot
XI. Nissan Rogue
XII. Hyundai Tucson

As you can see in the above given examples, the numbering of the outputs started at the third. There seems to be no problem with the numbers, but what about the letters?

**Frequently Asked Questions (FAQ)**

***What happens when you use type a or type A, which are represented by the letters of the English alphabet, and you go over the number 26?***
You continue counting by going back to the first letter, but this time, you double the letters. In the modern English alphabet, there are only 26 letters.

So, if you want to start with number "23", which represents the letter "w", and you have more than four items on your list, you will get the letters "aa" by the time the counting reaches the 27th.

This happens because the 26th letter is "z" and that would go to your fourth item. Since you have more than four items on the list and the last letter of the English alphabet is "z", you have to go back to letter "a" for your fifth item, and so on.

***Would you get an error if you start with 27 or beyond?***
No, you will not get an error. Your program will still run.

***Would the counting go back to number "1" which represents the letter "a"?***
Yes, but as mentioned earlier, the letters would be doubled this time around. To help you understand this concept further, here is an example for you to study:

```
< ! DOCTYPE html >
< html >
< head >
< title > This sample program shows you how an ordered list
using type a start 23 looks like < /title >
< /head >
< /body >
< ol type = " a "  start = " 23" >
< li > Toyota Camry < /li >
```

```
< li > Subaru Forester < /li >
< li > Lexus RX < /li >
< li > Chevrolet Impala < /li >
< li > Honda Civic </li >
< li > Subaru Outback < /li >
< li > Jeep Grand Cherokee < /li >
< li > Honda Pilot < /li >
< li > Nissan Rogue < /li >
< li > Hyundai Tucson < /li >
< /ol >
< /body >
< /html >
```

The output of the above given example should be as follows:

w. Toyota Camry
x. Subaru Forester
y. Lexus RX
z. Chevrolet Impala
aa. Honda Civic
ab. Subaru Outback
ac. Jeep Grand Cherokee
ad. Honda Pilot
ae. Nissan Rogue
af. Hyundai Tucson

How about if you wanted to start with a really large number like "1000"? Well, you will just keep going back to start. You will basically just go round and round the alphabet.

Consider the following example:

```
< ! DOCTYPE html >
< html >
< head >
< title > This sample program shows you how an ordered list
using type A start 1000 looks like < /title >
```

```
< /head >
< /body >
< ol type = " A " start = " 1000" >
< li > Toyota Camry < /li >
< li > Subaru Forester < /li >
< li > Lexus RX < /li >
< li > Chevrolet Impala < /li >
< li > Honda Civic </li >
< li > Subaru Outback < /li >
< li > Jeep Grand Cherokee < /li >
< li > Honda Pilot < /li >
< li > Nissan Rogue < /li >
< li > Hyundai Tucson < /li >
< /ol >
< /body >
< /html >
```

The output of the above given example should be as follows:

```
ALL. Toyota Camry
ALM. Subaru Forester
ALN. Lexus RX
ALO. Chevrolet Impala
ALP. Honda Civic
ALQ. Subaru Outback
ALR. Jeep Grand Cherokee
ALS. Honda Pilot
ALT. Nissan Rogue
ALU. Hyundai Tucson
```

# Unordered Lists

Unordered lists are collections of related items that do not have any special sequence or order. You can create an unordered list with the use of the tag <ul>. When you use this tag, all the items in your list will be marked with bullets.

To help you understand this concept further, you should take a look at the following example:

```
< ! DOCTYPE html >
< html >
< head >
< title > This sample program shows you how a basic unordered list looks like < /title >
< /head >
< /body >
< ul >
< li > Colt Python < /li >
< li > Desert Eagle < /li >
< li > Diamondback < /li >
< li > Glock < /li >
< li > Grendel </li >
< li > Mauser Model < /li >
< li > Pocket Pistols < /li >
< li > Ruger Old Army Revolvers < /li >
< li > Smith and Wesson < /li >
< li > Weatherby Vanguard < /li >
< /ul >
< /body >
< /html >
```

The output of the above given example should be as follows:

- Colt Python
- Desert Eagle
- Diamondback
- Glock

- Grendel
- Mauser Model
- Pocket Pistols
- Ruger Old Army Revolvers
- Smith and Wesson
- Weatherby Vanguard

## The Type Attribute

As the programmer, you are free to use the type attribute for the tag < ul > if you want. Its purpose is for specifying which type of bullet you prefer. If you do not specify a particular type, you would get a disc by default, just like what you got using the sample program shown above.

The following table shows you the type attributes that you can use for ordered lists:

| Type | Description |
|---|---|
| none | If you use this type, your list items would not be marked. |
| disc | If you use this type, your list items would be marked with regular bullets. |
| circle | If you use this type, your list items would be marked with circle bullets. |
| square | If you use this type, your list items would be marked with square bullets. |

To help you understand the functions of the list attributes for unordered lists, you should take a look at the following examples:

In this sample program, the type = " none " attribute is used:

```
< ! DOCTYPE html >
< html >
< head >
< title > This sample program shows you how an unordered
list using type none looks like < /title >
< /head >
< /body >
< ul type = " none " >
< li > Tyrion Lannister < /li >
< li > Daenerys Targaryen < /li >
< li > Arya Stark < /li >
< li > Jon Snow < /li >
< li > Sansa Stark </li >
< li > Cersei Lannister < /li >
< li > Joffrey Baratheon < /li >
< li > Jaime Lannister < /li >
< li > Brienne of Tarth < /li >
< li > Margaery Tyrell < /li >
< /ul >
< /body >
< /html >
```

The output of the above given example should be as follows:

Tyrion Lannister
Daenerys Targaryen
Arya Stark
Jon Snow
Sansa Stark
Cersei Lannister
Joffrey Baratheon
Jaime Lannister
Brienne of Tarth
Margaery Tyrell

In this sample program, the type = " disc " attribute is used:

```
< ! DOCTYPE html >
< html >
< head >
< title > This sample program shows you how an unordered
list using type disc looks like < /title >
< /head >
< /body >
< ul type = " disc " >
< li > Zeus < /li >
< li > Hera < /li >
< li > Poseidon < /li >
< li > Aphrodite < /li >
< li > Hades </li >
< li > Demeter < /li >
< li > Apollo < /li >
< li > Athena < /li >
< li > Artemis < /li >
< li > Hermes < /li >
< /ul >
< /body >
< /html >
```

The output of the above given example should be as follows:

- Zeus
- Hera
- Poseidon
- Aphrodite
- Hades
- Demeter
- Apollo
- Athena
- Artemis
- Hermes

In this sample program, the type = " circle " attribute is used:

```
< ! DOCTYPE html >
< html >
< head >
< title > This sample program shows you how an unordered
list using type circle looks like < /title >
< /head >
< /body >
< ul type = " circle " >
< li > Jupiter < /li >
< li > Juno < /li >
< li > Neptune < /li >
< li > Venus < /li >
< li > Pluto </li >
< li > Ceres < /li >
< li > Apollo < /li >
< li > Minerva < /li >
< li > Diana < /li >
< li > Mercury < /li >
< /ul >
< /body >
< /html >
```

The output of the above given example should be as follows:

- Jupiter
- Juno
- Neptune
- Venus
- Pluto
- Ceres
- Apollo
- Minerva
- Diana
- Mercury

In this sample program, the type = " square " attribute is used:

```
< ! DOCTYPE html >
< html >
< head >
< title > This sample program shows you how an unordered list using type square looks like < /title >
< /head >
< /body >
< ul type = " square " >
< li > Toyota Camry < /li >
< li > Subaru Forester < /li >
< li > Lexus RX < /li >
< li > Chevrolet Impala < /li >
< li > Honda Civic </li >
< li > Subaru Outback < /li >
< li > Jeep Grand Cherokee < /li >
< li > Honda Pilot < /li >
< li > Nissan Rogue < /li >
< li > Hyundai Tucson < /li >
< /ul >
< /body >
< /html >
```

The output of the above given example should be as follows:

- Toyota Camry
- Subaru Forester
- Lexus RX
- Chevrolet Impala
- Honda Civic
- Subaru Outback
- Jeep Grand Cherokee
- Honda Pilot
- Nissan Rogue
- Hyundai Tucson

# Definition Lists

Definition lists are supported by both XHTML and HTML. You can use these lists if you want your entries to be listed and sorted out just like they would appear in a dictionary.

Definition lists are recommended to be used for lists of terms, glossary, and other lists that show names and values.

In general, there are three tags used for definition lists:

< dl > - It is used to define the beginning of your list.
< dt > - It is used for terms.
< dd > - It is used for the definitions of the terms.

When you are done with the items in your list, you have to use </dl> to define its ending.

To help you understand this concept further, you should take a look at the following example:

```
< !DOCTYPE html >
< html >
< head >
< title > This is a sample program of an HTML and CSS
Definition List < /title >
< /head >
< body >
< h3 > A Sample Definition List < /h3 >
< dl >
< dt > < b > HTML < /b > < /dt >
< dd > It is an acronym for Hyper Text Markup Language < /dd >
< dt > < b > CSS < /b > < /dt >
< dd > It is an acronym for Cascading Style Sheets < /dd >
< /dl >
< /body >
< /html >
```

The output of the above given example should be as follows:

## A Sample Definition List

**HTML**

It is an acronym for Hyper Text Markup Language

**CSS**

It is an acronym for Cascading Style Sheets

# CHAPTER 7:
# HTML LINKS

Your web page can feature a variety of links that directly take the user to another web page. It can even direct the user to specific locations on your website. These links are called hyperlinks. They let your visitors navigate throughout your website by clicking on images, words, and/or phrases. You can create a hyperlink using any image or text you have on your web page.

## Text Links

In order for you to be able to link documents, you have to specify the links using the anchor tag <a>. Whatever is placed between the opening <a> and closing </a> anchor tags become part of a link. When visitors come to your website, they can click the link to be directed to the corresponding document.

The following syntax is for using the anchor tag:

< a href = " the URL of the document " . . . attributes – list >
the link text < /a >

To help you understand this concept further, you should take a look at the following example:

```
< !DOCTYPE html >
< html >
< head >
< title > This is a basic example of a link or hyperlink. <
/title>
< /head >
< body >
```

```
< a href = "https://www.sampleprogram.com" > This is an
example of a link. < /a >
< /body >
< /html >
```

The sample program shown above should yield the following
output:

This is an example of a link.

Here is another example:

```
< !DOCTYPE html >
< html >
< head >
< title > This is an example of a hyperlink. < /title>
< /head >
< body >
< p > Click here to go to the link < /p >
< a href = "https://www.sampleprogram.com" target =
"_self" > Sample Program Website < /a >
< /body >
< /html >
```

The sample program shown above should yield the following
output:

Click here to go to the link
Sample Program Website

If you click on the links in the sample programs shown above,
you will be directed to https://www.sampleprogram.com,
which is not really an existing link or website. It was only
used for the purpose of providing a sample for this book.

When you create a hyperlink, you can direct the visitor to
any web page. Most links, however, go to the homepage of
the website. You can simply provide the link or prompt the
visitor to click on it by adding some clickbait.

Then again, you have to organize your wording carefully, so you will not turn off the reader. Some readers tend to ignore the words "Click here" while others do not notice the text links if they do not contain the right keywords.

For example, if you want to link your About Us page, you can simply use the words "About Us" and put your hyperlink there instead of saying "Click here to know more about us."

### The Target Attribute
It is used for the purpose of specifying the location in which the linked document gets opened. As the programmer, you can use the following:

| Options | Descriptions |
|---|---|
| frame name | It loads your linked document on a frame that has a customized name. |
| _blank | It opens your linked document on another tab or window. |
| _parent | It opens your linked document in your parent frame. |
| _self | It opens your linked document within the same frame. |
| _top | It opens your linked document at the top level frameset or the entire browser window, regardless of the number of nested levels in the current frame. |

To help you learn more about these target attributes, here is a sample program that contains the different types:

87

```
< !DOCTYPE html >
< html >
< head >
< title > This sample program shows the different types of target
attributes used for text links. < /title>
< base href = "https://www.sampleprogram.com/">
< /head >
< body >
< p > You can click any of these links and you will arrive on the
same web page < /p >
< a href = "/html/index.htm" target = "_blank" > This one opens
in a new tab or window < /a >  |
< a href = "/html/index.htm" target = "_parent" > This one
opens in your parent frame < /a >  |
< a href = "/html/index.htm" target = "_self" > This one opens
within the same frame < /a >  |
< a href = "/html/index.htm" target = "_top" > This one opens
in the body < /a >
< /body >
< /html >
```

The sample program shown above should yield the following output:

You can click whichever one of these links and you will arrive on the same web page

This one opens in a new tab or window | This one opens in your parent frame | This one opens within the same frame | This one opens in the body

When you click any of the above given links, you will be directed to https://www.sampleprogram.com/html/index.htm, which in this book, is only a sample link. Its sole purpose is to demonstrate the linking of web pages.

## The Base Path

Keep in mind that you do not have to provide the complete URL for all the links you use for every time you link an HTML document to the same website. In fact, you may just eliminate it altogether if you go for the tag <base> in the header of the HTML document.

This tag gives the base path for each one of the links. Thus, the browser you use will simply concatenate the relative path towards the base path and produce the complete URL.

To help you understand how to use this tag further, as well as how to specify your base URL, you should take a look at the following example:

```
< !DOCTYPE html >
< html >
< head >
< title > This is another example of a hyperlink < /title>
< base href = "https://www.sampleprogram.com/">
< /head >
< body >
< p > Click this link < /p >
< a href = "/html/index.htm" target = "_blank" > A very easy
tutorial < /a >
< /body >
< /html >
```

The sample program shown above should yield the following output:

Click this link
A very easy tutorial

As you can see in this sample program, as well as the other sample program above it, there is no more need for you to type the entire URL. Instead of typing the very long URL https://www.sampleprogram.com/html/index.htm, you can simply type a href = "/html/index.htm, which is the important part of the URL. The visitor would be taken to the same web page.

As a programmer, it is crucial for you to look for shortcuts in order to make the most of your time and energy. You have to make your programs as short as possible, without negative affecting its output. You still have to get your desired output even if you have made your program shorter.

**Linking to Page Sections**
You may create links to certain sections of your web page through the use of name attributes. In general, there are two steps that you have to take to make this happen.

First, you have to create the necessary link to whichever location you want to arrive to within the web page. You can type the following:

```
< h1 > This is a basic example of a text link < a name = "top" >
< /a > < /h1 >
```

Next, you have to create the hyperlink in which you will link your document. You can type the following:

```
< a href = "/html/html_sample_text_link.htm#top" > Move to
top < /a >
```

When you run the above given code, you will get the following output:

Move to top
When you click on this link shown above, you will be directed to https://www.sampleprogram.com/html/html _sample_text_link.htm#top, which once again, is a non-

existent link and only used for the purpose of showing an example. If you use an actual link, you will be directed towards the top of the web page.

## Setting the Link Color

You may add colors to your links if you want. You can use the attributes alink, link, and vlink to set colors for your *active links*, *links*, and *visited links*, respectively.

To help you understand this concept better, you should take a look at the following sample program. Take note that you have to save it in test.htm. Then, you can open that in whatever web browser you want. You will then be able to learn how the attributes alink, link, and vlink function.

```
< !DOCTYPE html >
< html >
< head >
< title > This is another example of a hyperlink < /title>
< base href = "https://www.sampleprogram.com/">
< /head >
< body alink = "#54A250" link = "#040404" vlink = "#F40633"
>
< p > Click this link < /p >
< a href = "/html/index.htm" target = "_blank" > A very easy
tutorial < /a >
< /body >
< /html >
```

The sample program shown above should yield the following output:

Click this link
A very easy tutorial

Before you click on this link shown above, you have to check the color. You have to check it again once you activated it and once the target destination has been reached.

**Download Links**

If you want to create a text link, you can do that with HTML. In fact, text links are ideal to make files in PDF, ZIP, or DOC form downloadable. It is actually pretty simple. All you have to do is provide the URL of your file. You can use the following example as a guideline:

```
< !DOCTYPE html >
< html >
< head >
< title > This is an example for a hyperlink < /title >
< /head >
< a href = https://www.sampleprogram.com/page.pdf >
Click to download file < /a >
< /body >
< /html >
```

The above given example would result in the following output:

Click to download file

As you can see in the output, the text link "Click to download file" directs you to the page where the file is found and lets you download it with quickness and ease.

**The File Download Dialog Box**

You can actually give your visitors an option to click on a link to display a File Download box rather than show them the actual content right away. You simply have to use an HTTP header for the HTTP response.

Say, you want to make a certain file downloadable via a certain link, you may use the following syntax:

```perl
#! / usr / bin /perl
# This is an added HTTP header
print " Content – Type : application / octet – stream ;
name = \ " SampleFile \ " \ r \ n" ;
print " Content – Disposition : attachment ;
filename = \ " SampleFile \ " \ r \ n \ n" ;

# This opens your target file and lists down the contents such as
the following
open ( FILE, " < SampleFile " ) ;
while ( read ( FILE , $buffer , 100 ) ) {
        print ( " $buffer " ) ;
}
```

In the above given example, the name of the file is SampleFile. You can use this example as a guideline to help you write your program.

# Image Links

Texts are great for creating hypertext links and images are useful for web pages. In HTML, you can get the best of both worlds. You can use images as your hyperlinks. The process is simple and easy. You just have to put an image within the hyperlink.

You can use images, icons, or graphics. Just make sure that you do not violate any copyright rules. As much as possible, you should use your own images. If you cannot produce one, you can use free images from the Internet.

## Putting HTML Images on Web Pages

The command used to put images on a web page is constant. You have to use the same format each time you want to do this. As a programmer, you may want to put your images in the subdirectory "images". Here is the format that you have to use to place an image on your web page:

```
< img src = "image.png" alt = "some texts" width = 30 height = 30 >
```

Of course, the above given example is only a guideline. You can modify it depending on your file name and preferences for width and height.

## The Image Element Parameters

The following are the image element parameters that you have to keep in mind:

*img*. It stands for image. Also, it tells the web browser that an image would be shown on the web page. The image would appear on the exact place you put it in your image tag.

*<image name>.<suffix>*. The image name can be anything you want while the suffix can be any of the allowed image

formats: .gif, .png, .jpg, .jpeg, and .bmp. For example: sampleimage.png, imagetest.gif.

*src.* It stands for source. It is an attribute or a command within a command. It tells the web browser where it has to go to locate the image. Take note that it would be much easier to use a subdirectory named as "images" than to search for your images in random locations. By putting all your images in this subdirectory, you can simply call for them by using a subdirectory name such as /images/sampleimage.jpeg.

In addition, you can direct your source to another place on the Internet. For example, if you are using an image hosting website, you have to use the complete URL of your image such as in the following example: http://www.imagehostingwebsite.com/youraccount/sample image.jpg.

*alt.* It stands for alternate text. It tells the web browser that if it cannot locate the image, it can display a particular text. In addition, it informs visitors who cannot see the image what it is about. It shows up when the mouse is hovered over the image.

*<description text>.* It is where you place the text that describes the image. It is found within the body of the program.

*height.* It stands for the height of the image measured by pixels. You can define any height you want, but it has to be smaller than that of your web browser.

*width.* It stands for the width of the image measured by pixels. You can define any width you want, but it has to be smaller than that of your web browser.

## Image Formats

The following are the image formats that you can use for your image links:

*.png*. It is pronounced as ping and stands for Portable Network Graphic. It has partial transparency options. However, there are still browsers that do not display files that have this suffix.

*.gif*. It is pronounced as jif and stands for Graphics Interchange Format. It is a simple format that features a series of colored pixels or picture elements to form a picture. It is easily read by web browsers. It uses compression, but only when it is first made into such format.

*.jpg* or *jpeg*. It is pronounced as j-peg. The reason why there are two names for this format is because MAC and PC formats allow three and four letters after the dot. It stands for Joint Photographic Experts Group, which is the organization that developed it. This format is one of a kind because uses compression throughout its lifetime.

When your computer does not use an image in this format, it simply folds and stores it away. For instance, a certain picture can be shown at 10k bytes but stored at only 4k bytes. This is a great space saving technique. You get to save on valuable hard drive space. However, you also need more memory to unfold such image.

*.bmp*. It is pronounced as bimp and stands for bitmap. Bitmaps are images that computers produce and place for users. Although it is not likely for programmers to use bitmap for their images, some web browsers still allow it.

## Frequently Asked Questions (FAQs)

### *Is .gif really pronounced with a soft G?*

Yes, it is. You may argue that it could be otherwise since the Oxford English Dictionary accepts both hard and soft G pronunciations. Also, the letter G stands for the word 'graphic', which is obviously pronounced with a hard G. So, why should it be 'jif'?

The pronunciation of this popular image format has been a cause of debate for years. A little while ago, however, its creator, Steve Wilhite, set the record straight and said that the correct pronunciation is 'jif', with a soft G. The man who made .gif already said that it is 'jif', so you should just accept it as it is.

### *What about if you still cannot accept it? You have been so used to saying it with a hard G?!*

Well, you have to know about the rules of the pronunciation of the letter G. In essence, if the letter G is followed by a letter that is e, i, or y, its pronunciation would be soft. Some examples include the words "gin", "engine", "magic", "page", "vengeance", "generation", "gym", "astrology", and "Egypt".

On the other hand, if the letter G is followed by any other letter other than e, i, and y, its pronunciation would be hard. Consider the words "gazebo", "grass", "go", and "gloves". Some exceptions, however, are the words "give" and "gift".

### *Where can you get free images for your web page?*

You can get free images from libraries of stock photos. There are a lot of websites that offer these royalty-free images. Most websites that offer free images for commercial business purposes have a Creative Commons license. Creative Commons is a non-profit organization that accepts submissions of photos, videos, and audio files.

Some of the websites you can visit to search for free images include Wikimedia.org, Flickr, Pixabay, FreeDigitalPhotos.net, Deviant Art, BigFoto.com, and Openclipart.org.

***Is giving credit the same as asking for permission? In other words, can you use a certain image, acknowledge its owner, and not violate any rules on copyright?***
No. Unless the owner of the image file specifically said that anyone can use his or her work as long as that person gives him or her credit, you need to talk to the owner and ask for permission. Basically, it is not enough to just mention the name of the owner and provide a link to the original file.

You should not assume that there would not be any copyright infringements if you credit the owner or author. Sadly, there are so many people who are misinformed. They make the classic mistake of merely crediting the author and not actually contacting him or her to ask for permission.

If you do not want to be in any copyright trouble, you should probably just play it safe and either use your own image file or get one from a website that offers stock photos.

**Turning Images Into Links**
When you create hypertext links, all you get are blue words with links connected to them. If you want to make your images active or clickable, you have to provide them with hypertext links. You can do that by using the following format:

< a href = "https://www.sampleprogram.com" > < img src = "homepageimage.gif " alt = "home" > < /a >

In the above given example, fictitious URLs were once again used to serve as guidelines.

When you put an image tag in a location where you usually put words, you get an image link instead of a mere text link.

Instead of words becoming blue, it is the borders of the image that turn blue. Well, this can actually be any color you want to set your web page to. The default color is usually blue.

If you do not like the borders because they annoy you or you just prefer no borders, you can make them disappear by using the following CSS codes:

```
< img style = "border : none ;"  src = "homepageimage.gif" alt
= "home" >
```

Take note that homepageimage.gif is just an example. You have to use your own link for this part. When you add CSS codes that denote the non-inclusion of borders, you can enjoy a border-free image on your web page.

However, if you like borders and you actually want the border to get bigger, you can modify the code into something like the following:

```
< img style = "border : 55px solid blue ;" src =
"homepageimage.gif" alt = "home" >
```

You can see if your image is now active by hovering over it. Take note that you should just move the pointer over the image and not click on it.

In case your image does not become viewable for whatever reason, it would be great to add an alternate text informing the user where your link goes.

It is not really that difficult to create image links. You just have to provide the URLs of your website and location of your image file. You also have to indicate if you would like to see a border or not.

To help you understand this concept further, you should take a look at the following example:

```
< !DOCTYPE html >
< html >
< head >
< title > This is an example of an image hyperlink < /title>
< /head >
< body >
< p > Click this link < /p >
< a href = "https://www.sampleprogram.com" target = "_self" >
       < img src = "/images/logo.jpg" alt = "Sample Program"
border = "0"/ >
< /a >
< /body >
< /html >
```

The sample program shown above would produce an image link as its output. When you click on this link, you would be directed to the homepage of the sample website used in the program.

**Mouse-Sensitive Images**
Both XHTML and HTML standards offer a feature that allows you to embed a variety of links inside one image. This would depend on the coordinates available on this image. When you connect different links to different coordinates, you can click on different locations on the image to open it.

The image becomes mouse-sensitive. It becomes an image map. In general, there are a couple of ways on how to create an image map: server-side and client-side.

A server-side image map is made with the <img> tag attribute ismap. It requires access to related image-map processing applications and a server. A client-side image map is made with the <img> tag attribute usemap, along with the <area> and <map> tags.

## Server-Side Image Maps

If you choose to create a server-side image map, you simply have to place the image within a hyperlink and then use the attribute *ismap* to activate or enable it.

When you click anywhere on the image, your browser passes the coordinates of your mouse pointer as well as the URL that you used. Your server uses the coordinates of the mouse pointer to identify which document it would send back to the web browser.

When you use ismap, the attribute href of the <a> tag has to have the URL of the server application, such as a PHP or CGI script, in order for it to be able to read the passed coordinates and then process the request.

Mouse position coordinates refer to the screen pixels. When you count these pixels, you start at the upper left portion or at (0,0).

## Client-Side Image Maps

The attribute *usemap* enables these images. Its value is necessary to create image tags and link maps. <area> and <map> tags define the image coordinates as well as their links.

## The Coordinate System

The shape you use determines the value of your coordinates. Keep in mind that every coordinate is relative to the upper left portion of the image (0,0). Every shape has a URL. If you want to learn about the coordinates of various positions, you can use an image software.

The following are the coordinates for rectangles, circles, and polygons:

*rect* = $x_1, y_1, x_2, y_2$
In the upper left portion, you will find the $x_1$ and $y_1$ coordinates. In the lower right portion, you will find the $x_2$ and $y_2$ coordinates.

*circle* = $x_o, y_o$, *radius*
At the center, you will find the $x_c$ and $y_c$ coordinates. Radius refers to the radius of the circle.

*poly* = $x_1, y_1, x_2, y_2, x_3, y_3, \ldots x_n, y_n$
The points or vertices of the polygon are defined by the x and y pairs.

In the above given example, the name of the file is SampleFile. You can use this example as a guideline to help you write your program.

# Email Links

You may think that it is difficult to place HTML email links on web pages, but it is actually very easy. However, it is not advisable to do it because it can result in spamming problems. You can receive unnecessary spam messages on your email.

So, unless you want to purposely receive these kinds of emails, you should probably avoid using email links on your web pages. There are certain individuals who use specific programs to collect such emails and then use them to spam accounts.

If you want visitors to send you emails, you can use an HTML form to gather their data. Then, you can use CGI or PHP scripts to send out emails.

For example, you can use the link https://www.sampleprogram.com/about/contact_us.htm to collect the necessary data. Of course, you need to turn it into a hyperlink. You can use Contact Us or Email Us for this purpose.

When a visitor of your website clicks on the link, he will be directed to the web page wherein he can fill up the form. You can use this form to collect user feedback or user information. Then, you can use a CGI program to get such data and send it to your email account.

## Email Tags

When you use the tag <a>, you can choose which email address you want your emails to be sent to. You simply have to type mailto:email address with the href attribute.

You have to use the following syntax if you want to use mailto rather than http:

```
< a href = "mailto:wdd@sampleprogram.com"  > Click to
send an email < /a >
```

When you run the above given code, you would get the
following output:

Click to send an email

When a user clicks on the link, an email client will be
launched. It can be Outlook Express, Lotus Notes, etc.
However, if the user does not have any email client installed
on his computer, he will not be able to send an email using
this link.

**Default Settings**

If you want to have a default email body and email subject
with an email address, you can use the following example as
a guide:

```
<a
href="mailto:wdd@sampleprogram.com?subject=Feedback&
body=Message">
Click to send feedback
</a>
```

A link, which the visitor can use to send an email, would then
be generated.

# CHAPTER 8:
# CSS COLOR

## Fundamentals

You can easily make your pages look brighter and livelier by using good colors and color combinations. Then again, you have to know how to specify them. You also have to be familiar with the color terminologies. See to it that you use background colors and contrast to your advantage.

### Foreground Color
You can specify text colors within elements through the color property. In fact, you can specify colors using RGB values, color names, and hex codes.

RGB values express colors according to the amount of red, green, and blue they contain. RGB basically stands for red, green, and blue. Color names are the names of the colors that humans and browsers easily recognize. Hex codes refer to the six-digit codes representing the amount of red, green, and blue a color has. A hash or pound sign ( # ) comes before it.

### Background Color
Every HTML element is treated by CSS as if it is shown inside a box. Background-color sets which color is used for the background of this box. Just like with foreground colors, you can specific which colors you want by using RGB values, color names, and hex codes.

What happens if you do not specify any background color? Your background will be transparent unless you choose a particular color for it.

By default, a white background is used on browser windows. Nevertheless, you are free to set a specific background color for your windows. You can use the property background-color on the element <body>. If you want to make your text more readable, you can separate it from the edge of the box through the use of padding.

**Color Basics**
All the colors you see on your computer screen are created by combining the colors red, green, and blue. If you want to search for a particular color, you can use color pickers. Image editing programs such as Photoshop feature these tools.

In essence, your computer monitor is composed of very small squares known as pixels. These pixels can be seen by the naked eye, but you have to look very closely at your screen.

When your computer is turned off, you only see the blackness because there is no light present. Once you turn it on, you will be able to see the pixels that are of different colors. These pixels create images and texts.

*RGB Values*
The values used to represent red, green, and blue range from 0 to 255.

*Color Names*
Predefined names represent colors, although they are limited.

*Hex Codes*
Hexadecimal codes are also used for the values that represent red, green, and blue.

*Hue*
It is near the colloquial impression of color.

*Brightness*
Also referred to as value, it refers to the amount of black present in a particular color. The color tends to be very dark

at minimum brightness. The color does not contain any black at maximum brightness.

### Saturation

It refers to how much gray is present in a particular color. The color is mostly gray at minimum saturation. The color does not contain any gray at maximum saturation.

Here is a sample program:

```
< !DOCTYPE html >
< html >
< head >
< style >
body {
    color : blue ;
}

h1 {
    color : green ;
}
< /style >
< /head >
< body >

< h1 > This is an example of a heading < /h1 >
< p > This is a sample text. It is blue because the default color is blue. If you wish to change the color, you have to edit the body selector. < /p >

< /body >
< /html >
```

When you run it, you would get the following output:

# This is an example of a heading

This is a sample text. It is blue because the default color is blue. If you wish to change the color, you have to edit the body selector.

# Related Elements

Do not forget to specify the contrast and opacity.

## Contrast

See to it that there is sufficient contrast for your text to be legible when you choose background and foreground colors.

### High Contrast

If there is a high contrast between the background and the foreground colors, the text becomes easier to read. However, you should not use too much contrast because it can cause the text to be difficult to read.

### Medium Contrast

You can improve the readability of a text when you reduce its contrast. This is especially ideal if you have long texts. You can use a white background and a dark gray text or a dark background and an off white text to reduce the contrast.

### Low Contrast

If there is a low contrast between the background and the foreground colors, the text becomes more difficult to read. Lack of contrast is a common problem for people with color blindness and visual impairments. It also makes reading text on handheld devices difficult if you are outdoors and the sunlight reflects on your screen. You can also experience the same problem if you are using a low quality monitor.

## Opacity

This property lets you specify which element opacity and child element you want to have. You can choose any value from 0.0 to 1.0. For example, if you want to have 15% opacity, you have to choose 0.15.

# CHAPTER 9:
# CSS TEXT

## Typeface

In general, there are two classifications of properties that let you control how your text appears. First, there is the one that has a direct effect on the font that you use. It affects its appearance and typeface. Then, there is the one that lets you use whatever font you want as well as control the text color and spacing between the letters and words, and still has the same effect on your text.

Keep in mind that the text formatting that you have can have a huge effect on the readability of your pages.

### Typeface Terminology

#### *Monospace*
All the letters in a fixed-width or monospace font have the same width. The letters in a non-monospace font, on the other hand, have varying widths.

#### *Weight*
The weight of fonts is classified into light, medium, bold, and black. They do not only add emphasis. They also affect the number of whitespaces and amount of contrast on the page.

#### *Stretch*
The stretch is classified into condensed, regular, and extended. Narrow or condensed font versions feature thin letters that are close to each other. Expanded font versions have thicker letters that are far from each other.

### Style

Style can be normal, italic, or oblique. An italic font has a cursive aspect to its lettering while an oblique font puts the normal style on an angle.

### Selecting a Typeface

When it comes to selecting a typeface, you have to take your browser into consideration. Remember that it will only display the typeface if it is installed in the computer.

Because of this, most websites go for small sets of typefaces that are commonly installed on computers. Nevertheless, there are certain techniques you can use if you wish to bypass such limitation.

You can specify several typefaces and produce an order of preference. This is known as the font stack. It is recommended that you include the generic name of the font that you like after selecting a particular typeface.

### Sans-Serif

These fonts feature straight ends and a very clean design.

### Serif

These fonts feature additional details at the ends of the primary letter strokes. Such details are called serifs.

### Fantasy

These fonts are decorative and ideal for titles. They are not ideal for bodies of text.

### Cursive

These fonts may have joining strokes and other cursive characteristics like handwriting styles.

## More Selections of Typefaces

You can use certain techniques to obtain more fonts. However, you have to take note that typefaces tend to be copyrighted. Thus, the techniques you can use are often limited by their licenses.

| Font-Family | Font-Face | Service-Based Font-Face |
|---|---|---|
| You need to have the typeface installed on your computer. You can use CSS to specific this typeface. | If the font is not installed on your computer, you can use CSS to find out where you can download it. | You can gain access to more fonts by using commercial services. |
| **Issues** | | |
| Your choices of typefaces are limited. | You have to download your font file, causing your web page to slow down. | You have to pay fees in order to cover the licenses that are purchased from the font foundries. |
| **Licensing** | | |
| There aren't any issues with regard to licensing because it is not you who distributes the typeface. | The license for using the font has to permit distribution with the use of font-face. | Service deals with issues on licensing associated with the individuals who created the font. |
| **Choice of Typefaces** | | |
| The choice of typefaces is limited due to the fact that the fonts have to be installed on the computer. | The choice is limited due to the fact that only a few typefaces can be distributed freely. | Every service offers a unique choice of fonts depending on their contract or agreement with the font foundries. |

You can use a PC or a Mac to design typefaces. However, you should keep in mind that the appearance of the typeface can appear differently on these devices. If you design using a Mac, you have to look at how the typefaces appear on a PC since it tends to render less smoothly. If you design using a PC, you have no problem because it would still look good on a Mac.

# Properties

The following are some of the text properties that you have to learn if you want to successfully write programs:

## Text Alignment
You can use text-align to set your text's horizontal alignment. You can make it left aligned, right aligned, justified, or centered.

Here is an example:

```
< !DOCTYPE html >
< html >
< head >
< style >
h1 {
   text - align : center ;
}

h2 {
   text - align : left ;
}

h3 {
   text - align :  right ;
}
< /style >
< /head >
< body >
< h1 > Sample Centered Heading < /h1 >
< h2 > Sample Left Aligned Heading < /h2 >
< h3 > Sample Right Aligned Heading < /h3 >
< p > These three sample headings show three different text alignments. < / p >
< /body >
< /html >
```

When you run the above given program, you will get the following output:

# Sample Centered Heading

# Sample Left Aligned Heading

# Sample Right Aligned Heading

These three sample headings show three different text alignments.

As you can see in the example, the text-align property justify is not used. If you decide to use it, however, you can expect every line of your text to be stretched out. Its purpose is to show equal width as well as straight left and right margins.

**Text Decoration**

You can use text-decoration to remove or set decorations from your text. Likewise, you can use text-decoration: none; if you wish to remove an underline from a link.

Take a look at the following sample programs:

```
< !DOCTYPE html >
< html >
< head >
< style >
a {
   text - decoration : none ;
}
< /style >
< /head >
< body >
```

114

```
< p > This link has no underline: < a href =
"https://www.sampleprogram.com" >Sample Text < /a > <
/p >
< /body >
< /html >
```

This first example shows a text link without an underline.
You should get the following output:

This link has no underline: Sample Text

However, if you want your text to be underlined, you have to
declare it. You may also use other text decorations such as
line-through.

```
< !DOCTYPE html >
< html >
< head >
< style >
h1 {
    text - decoration : line-through ;
}

h2 {
    text - decoration : underline ;
}
< /style >
< /head >
< body >
< h1 > This is an example of a strikethrough text < /h1 >
< h2 > This is an example of an underlined text < /h2 >
< /body >
< /html >
```

When you run this program, you would see the following output:

## ~~This is an example of a strikethrough text~~
## <u>This is an example of an underlined text</u>

**Text Transformation**

You can use text-transform if you wish to specify lowercase and uppercase letters in your text. You can make the entire word lowercase or uppercase. You can also simply capitalize the first letter.

Here is a sample program:

```
< !DOCTYPE html >
< html >
< head >
< style >
p.uppercase {
    text - transform : uppercase ;
}
p.lowercase {
    text - transform : lowercase ;
}
p.capitalize {
    text - transform : capitalize ;
}
< /style >
< /head >
< body >
< p class = "uppercase" > A sample text < /p >
< p class = "lowercase" > A sample text < /p >
< p class = "capitalize" > A sample text < /p >
< /body >
< /html >
```

116

When you run this program, you would see the following output:

```
A SAMPLE TEXT
a sample text
A Sample Text
```

# CONCLUSION

Thank you again for downloading this book!

I hope this book was able to help you learn how to use HTML and CSS.

The next step is to apply what you have learned from this book.

Finally, if you enjoyed this book, then I'd like to ask you for a favor, would you be kind enough to leave a review for this book on Amazon? It'd be greatly appreciated!

Click here to leave a review for this book on Amazon!

Thank you and good luck!

# DID YOU ENJOY THIS BOOK?

I want to thank you for purchasing and reading this book. I really hope you got a lot out of it.

Can I ask a quick favor though?

If you enjoyed this book I would really appreciate it if you could leave me a positive review on Amazon.

I love getting feedback from my customers and reviews on Amazon really do make a difference. I read all my reviews and would really appreciate your thoughts.

Thanks so much.
Micheal Knapp

p.s. Please go directly to the book on Amazon and leave your review.

47806373R00069

Made in the USA
San Bernardino, CA
08 April 2017